First You Sit on the Floor

A Guide to Developing a Youth Theatre Troupe

Michael Burns

HEINEMANN ■ Portsmouth, NH

Heinemann
A division of Reed Elsevier Inc.
361 Hanover Street
Portsmouth, NH 03801–3912
www.heinemanndrama.com

Offices and agents throughout the world

© 2002 by Michael G. Burns

Library of Congress Cataloging-in-Publication Data
Burns, Michael, 1957–
    First you sit on the floor : a guide to developing a youth theatre troupe / Michael Burns.
        p. cm.
    Includes bibliographical references.
    ISBN 0-325-00458-7 (alk. paper)
    1. College and school drama.   2. Amateur theater—Production and direction.   I. Title.

PN3178.P7 B87 2002
792'.022—dc21   2002004346

Editor: Lisa A. Barnett
Production: Vicki Kasabian
Cover design: Jenny Jensen Greenleaf
Author photo: Kate Burns
Typesetter: Kim Arney Mulcahy
Manufacturing: Jamie Carter

Printed in the United States of America on acid-free paper
06   05   04   03   02   DA   1   2   3   4   5

Dedicated to Helen Foley,
who called her students birds,
and watched them fly.

ontents

Caveat

If you read this book, and decide to go on, may the gods be with you. Remember, as the man said in *Shakespeare in Love:* it all works out somehow—exactly how is something of a mystery. Remember also that part of the mystery is that what works out may have little to do with your expectations. The following two vignettes are for your consideration.

Vignette 1

The first grader is given a large piece of brown paper toweling, with a sensually delightful glop of wintergreen-scented paste on it, a pile of fat crayons, several scraps of colored construction paper, and a piece of white paper with a photocopied outline of a bird. Before the classroom teacher has even finished passing out all the materials, this young artist has engaged joyously in improvisation, transforming the brown paper toweling and scraps of construction paper into a three-cornered hat, complete with feather "macaroni," and covering the paper with the bird on it with a riot of expressive color. Then, she is shocked, shamed, and disappointed to find herself being "spoken to strictly" (the child calls it being yelled at) *about coloring in the lines and following instructions! The paper was for a* project, *not to make a* hat *with!* The student has done everything wrong! Shame!

Shame. . . .

Vignette 2

Principal: *Welcome to the faculty! I'm so glad you've joined us. In addition to your classroom duties, I'd like to offer you the opportunity to develop our annual orchestra concert! This, as I am sure you realize, is quite an honor!*

New Teacher: *Well, I'm flattered, but beyond a few piano lessons and singing in the youth choir at church, I really have no musical training . . .*

Principal: *Quite all right! Quite all right! We have a wonderfully talented group of kids, and I know you'll do beautifully with them . . . say, something by Beethoven? The Ninth Symphony, perhaps?*

New Teacher: *The Ninth Symphony? Really, sir, with its mix of instrumental and choral work of an advanced nature—*

Principal: *It will sound delightful, no? We have a closet under the stage with some instruments—at least I think we do—just see if you can post a flier or something for auditions, or whatever it is you creative people do, and I'm sure you'll be a big hit!*

New Teacher: *But, haven't the children their own instruments? Who gives them instrumental lessons?*

Principal: (With a blank look) *Lessons? Why would they need those?*

reface

Theatre, an art, an undertaking, and a way of life, is, by its very nature, life-affirming, spiritual, bawdy, tragic, comic, sublime, ridiculous, wise, and foolish. So are adolescents, and so, of course, are adults. Theatre is a reflection of that which is sacred in us.

The second of the two vignettes on the previous pages is a little scene that would probably never take place. Throughout the public education system, it is understood that music demands instruction, years of practice, and rehearsal. This is offered in public schools as a matter of course. Similarly, art is well defined as curriculum, and many high schools have state-of-the-art equipment and arts faculties. Theatre and dance, however, are the bastard children of the arts. In primary schools, the "school play" is often a thinly disguised concert with some awkward readings attached, and in secondary school, the born troupers are relegated to an underfunded drama club. This is a tragedy, because theatre enriches all of the seven types of intelligence: linguistic, math/logic, aesthetic, kinetic/kinesthetic, interpersonal, intrapersonal, and musical/rhythmic.

Theatre heals, informs, entertains, and lifts up. Although the audience is its raison d'etre, its primary beneficiary is not necessarily the audience. There are those who must perform. It is in their nature as surely as the born athlete must run, or the bird must fly.

By its very nature, theatre is a teaching medium. It is an ideal medium for working with adolescents, especially those who bear the blessing/curse of the performer, in a way that will inform and transform them.

Theatre is *rotten* employment. Once upon a time, in the pre-electronic age, there was work for performers; every town in early twentieth-century America, for example, had its vaudeville house, and thousands of troupers (among them Ira Livingston, my grandfather) journeyed across the land, with their bird whistles, baggy pants, musical saws, harmonicas, hand-copied joke routines, and dreams. The people loved them. And, oddly, the people hated them: since time immemorial, the actor has been maligned as rogue, thief, whore; the farmer naturally distrusts and fears the wanderer.

Today, vaudeville is gone, a handful of performers create electronic entertainment for millions, and the vast majority of born performers are forced to sublimate their nature or to compromise their lifestyles to approximate some semblance of the life they *should* lead—they are amateurs. In the schools, these children of Dionysus are obvious to the trained eye. Sadly, these kids are often as misunderstood as their spiritual progenitors were. Their essential *otherness* makes them suspect. Their shenanigans are perceived as danger signs rather than signs of a gift, and they are often consigned to the ranks of the "bad kids."

Within this book, "prevention" as a field, specifically substance abuse prevention, will be the source of examples. Ironically, the author believes that the very term *prevention*, when applied to adolescents, is oxymoronic. In our culture the damage that leads to self-medication is done long before junior high school. We can intervene, but not prevent. Perhaps we should be talking about *interruption*, and hope that if we can help our young people discover, celebrate, and enrich their own real selves, if we can assist them in finding their own creativity and walk them down the path that leads to the joy of creation, the need for chemical or other anesthetics will be lessened. Further, if we can truly educate them about the choices they make when they self-medicate, we may in some cases hasten the day when individual youths seek help for their addictions.

If you work with youth, you already know that a certain number of those you work with go on to be adults with rich and wonderful lives, and some go on to be fairly miserable. You probably have discovered that you cannot predict which youths will end up in which state. What you *can* do is try to make their here-and-now experience with you enriching and uplifting. You can try to give them tools to use later. Perhaps most important, you can give them love and respect, two commodities young people *need*, in vast quantities. As for the rest—well, if you do already work with youth, you know you aren't really doing it for *them* so much as you are for yourself. The joy is in the journey. If it is the case that this book expands your knowledge, both theoretical and practical, of theatre as a medium for working with kids, then it has served its purpose well.

Enjoy.

A cknowledgments

ots of people helped make this book. I am thankful to all of them, named or unnamed here. Ken Klotz and Sally Stebbins at Skidmore College University Without Walls helped conceive this project and nurtured its early growth. My wife, Susan DeWolfe Burns, a gifted teacher, self-described "theatre widow," diplomatic critic, and my most ardent supporter, has helped in myriad ways large and small for years. Thanks, Susie. Thanks also to George Morrison, a great acting teacher, for putting up with a much younger me, and to David Shepherd, another very powerful early influence on my work, for sharing his unique and relentless pursuit of group creativity in its myriad forms. Thanks to my children, Josh, Kate, Tasha, and Willow, for hundreds of things. Thanks to Dr. Michael Tucker for being a cheerleader and gadfly. Thanks to Byron Nilsson, for agreement and amplification. Thanks to the excellent editors at Heinemann, Lisa Barnett and Vicki Kasabian. Thanks to Ellen Burns, my mom, who has always encouraged my work. Last but not least, thanks to all the young people I've worked with over the years, for all the joy.

▟ First You Sit on the Floor

ardboard signs and homemade props lie scattered about a bare stage in a college lecture hall, lit by crude lighting instruments. Three teenage girls in rubber pig masks "smoke" cardboard cigars, coughing and snorting. One of the masked girls speaks: "All right, boys, we have to *sell* the *product*! What are we going to use?" Another answers: "*sex*!" Four hundred high school students attending a prevention conference laugh appreciatively. This is a day in the life of the Spaha theatre group, one of many such groups that have performed in and around schools throughout the country.

Youth theatre is well established as a way to reach young audiences with a strong prevention message. Productions that go beyond mere "two-chair role-play" incorporate simple lighting and sound, costume fragments, props, and a transformational approach to staging that owes much to the Living Newspaper, a form of agitprop drama imported from Russia by the Federal Theatre during the Great Depression; the alternative theatre of the sixties and seventies, and the many improv troupes that gained popularity in the latter half of the twentieth century.

The following lays out a course of action for those in the human services and education fields who want to develop a program to dramatize issues of importance to youth and families as part of a prevention education effort.

The kind of theatre herein described is sometimes erroneously referred to as avant-garde by educational or human service professionals who are unfamiliar with the centuries-old tradition of non-scripted theatre in our culture. Those who wish to develop such a program may find they must first deal with the prejudices of their colleagues who distrust an improvisational approach. Indeed, many theatre people are somewhat prejudiced against nonscripted theatre (Fox 1991). Yet there is no doubt that nonscripted theatre, from the commedia (and even before) through the work of Second City and its descendants, has played an important role in the development of our society's theatrical milieu. Consider the impact of the Second City alone on the entertainment world in America: from that small improv troupe came an awe-inspiring number of stellar talents, including Mike Nichols, Elaine May, Shelley Berman, Barbara Harris, Ed Asner, Dan Ackroyd, John Belushi, Jack Burns, Avery Schreiber, John Candy, Robin Duke, Valerie Harper, Eugene Levy, Shelley Long, Andrea Martin, Bill Murray, Gilda Radner, David Mamet, Robert Klein . . . the list goes on and on (McCrohan 1987, 12). Clearly there is something in the method of this troupe that brings out talent!

Note that included in the list are playwrights, producers, directors, and actors, as well as stand-up comedians. The immediacy of improvisation, which in its urgency forces the actor to integrate the functions of actor, director, and playwright (as well as comic, occasionally) into the immediate moment may account for the diversity of talent that continues to spring from Second City.

It is important to stress at the start that the work described in this book, while intended to be helpful and, in a broad sense, therapeutic for the youths involved, is not therapy or psychodrama. In fact, a constant challenge when working with young people who may have been affected by the real-life experience of a given topic, for example, alcoholism, is that the psychodramatic experience may present itself in the course of the development of the piece, and correct handling of such a situation is critical.

Psychodrama is an intensely powerful modality, and, while it is in the nature of those in the helping profession to want to help someone work through a strong emotion, encouraging an individual to continue working on a scene or situation that is taking on the characteristics of psychodramatic probing is irresponsible. Surgery should be left to surgeons! In all work with young people in theatre, the first rule is "Safety first." We will return to the topic of psychodrama later.

Presentations on alcoholism/substance abuse will serve as examples throughout this piece. However, the techniques described herein can effectively carry any one of a number of positive messages to young people. I write this after successfully developing theatre pieces on subjects as diverse as respect for the differently abled, the HIV epidemic, child sexual abuse prevention and reporting, and teen pregnancy. I've also worked with kids to adapt fairy tales such as "The Ugly Duckling" and my own "The Prince Who Ate Tomorrow Cakes," purely for the joy of making theatre with kids—that, in my opinion, is where the potent medicine lurks, not necessarily in the message of a given piece. In other words, the medium is the magic.

Before beginning a youth theatre project, you must answer several questions. The first, while perhaps the most obvious, is of critical importance.

Why Do You Want to Develop a Youth Theatre?

To put this another way: What *kind* of youth theatre do you want, and why?

Before you answer, I would advise you to go rent three movies and watch them. First, Branagh's *A Midwinter's Tale* (1995). Second, *Waiting for Guffman* (1997). Third, *Shakespeare in Love* (1998). If you watch these brilliant depictions of the joy and insanity of the performer's life and still want to start a troupe, you are indeed right for the job. Now let's look at specific answers to the "why" question.

There may be several answers. Certainly peer role-play is an effective tool for disseminating factual information to youth. However, in my opinion, the primary goal of youth theatre should *not* be the dissemination of information to a wider audience, unless it is part of a larger whole, a program incorporating several training/ education experiences in a coordinated fashion. In prevention education, a wider, experiential approach is far more effective than a one-shot presentation (OSAP 1990a, 44). Certainly a theatre piece may be developed with an accompanying lesson plan or study guide for audience/classroom discussion after the performance. This, combined with dissemination of written material and more conventional audiovisual presentation of information, *might* constitute an effective package.

The primary goal of the development of a youth theatre program should be the education, empowerment, and training of the *actors*. At all times the focus of the youth theatre program should be on *process*, rather than *product*. This isn't easy: by its very nature, the theatrical process works for that golden moment when the curtain goes up.

There are many practitioners who have made important and valuable contributions in developing interactive social theatre as a tool in human services. Jonathan Fox, Augusto Boal, Michael Rohd, and others have published wonderful and helpful books and articles on facilitated, interactive theatre as a medium for social change. In this book I propose that a less interactive, less facilitated, more presentational theatre of youths—with more of what Aristotle called "spectacle" (Aristotle 1978, 13) and less of the trappings of a human services presentation—is in fact a valid and important way to go. I am proposing that you build a troupe whose primary focus is putting on *shows*, even if (especially if) *your* primary focus is the kind of prevention work that usually calls for *presentations*. Why?

Here's an old joke of questionable taste: What's the difference between Brussels sprouts and boogers? Answer: Kids *will* eat boogers. Simply: kids like shows, and they love to build them. They tend to be leery of and avoid presentations, unless said presentations are relieving them of an even more dismal classroom experience. So, a rule of thumb: the presentation that works beautifully during the school day in an assembly will tend to flop if presented to a "volunteer" audience of youths after school.

According to Dale's Cone of Learning, students achieve a 90 percent retention rate when actually doing, or simulating, an activity, as opposed to a mere 10 percent retention rate with lecture or reading material (Wiman and Meierhenry 1969). *Doing*—actively taking part in a creative process—is the key to the rich educational experience a youth theatre program offers.

If you successfully start a youth theatre, chances are that requests for performances will come rolling in from near and far. This is due to the hunger that exists in schools and agencies for *good* presentations, by youth for youth; as you probably know, there is a lot of mediocre stuff out there! It will then be important to book your troupe with the criterion of the good of the youthful actors in the forefront of your mind at all times, and not to become carried away by success. It's OK to turn down an offer.

The kind of program outlined in this document will accomplish the following for a group of young people: provide membership in a group with strong interpersonal bonds, enhance interpersonal communication skills, heighten individual members' awareness of the topic area(s) covered by the troupe, encourage creative problem solving, and teach techniques for identifying limiting paradigms. It will also provide them with a level of skill in, and knowledge of, improvisational theatre, thereby increasing their knowledge of dramatic structure and presentation skills. It will encourage them to create a living work of art.

Such work is not a magic pill, but it's really good for kids. It may be that *you*, who after all are reading this, already know this, but you have to convince another adult, perhaps a boss, or a funding source, or a parent, that in fact this youth theatre stuff is good and healthy, just like sports. The following thoughts are presented as tools for you to use in this justification.

Let's go back to Psych 101 for a moment, shall we? Remember Maslov, and that pyramid of his? We all want to reach the tippy-top, transcendence, or so they told us back in the lecture hall. If you consider the previous list of advantages to your student participants in light of Maslov's hierarchy of needs (Gleitman 1991, 732–37), you will see that the process outlined herein addresses the safety/affiliation needs by providing a group with strong bonds. It addresses the esteem/cognitive needs by teaching communication and problem-solving skills. Clearly it addresses the aesthetic need of the participants, since it involves developing an appreciation for and ability to construct an art form. It is the opinion of the author based on years of conversations with student actors that it will assist your actors on their path toward self-actualization and even, perhaps, transcendence, or "peak experiences."

If this is the case, then perhaps the key to the success of this kind of endeavor in prevention is that it combines knowledge of the dangers of substance abuse with the personal growth that helps eliminate the need for the anesthetic qualities of alcohol and other substances. But this growth cannot take place unless the most basic needs of your troupe's members are being met. Those who are in the greatest pain—in other words, those from the highest risk environments or those who have already crossed the threshold into abusive use/addiction—will not be able to take part in your work after a brave beginning; they will either drop out or, hopefully, be lucky enough to be referred to appropriate help by you. I have referred students to professional help for bulimia, aftereffects of rape, alcoholism/addiction, and child sexual abuse. Please don't view these cases—your "dropouts"—as your failures; they are indeed your successes.

In other words, this kind of program will not "fix" the participants. Members of companies that focus on alcohol and substance abuse issues have all too often been observed to drink in a high-risk fashion. However, if a young person chooses to be abstinent, such a program will reinforce that choice. Presumably if drinking/substance abuse becomes a problem in the life of a young person who takes part in such an activity, a knowledge of progression and symptoms of addictions *may* serve to raise the bottom for that young person, giving him enough information to recognize his problem in its early stages. On the "cover your butt" side of things, you should go on record early on stating so. This will later serve you, when a shocked administrator discovers that your star actor was arrested for DWI.

How Much Time Do You Have to Commit to the Project?

Developing a successful youth theatre troupe is a time-consuming and demanding proposition. Being clear on the amount of time required for the project from the very start is of critical importance. Ideally, you should be able to commit at least six to eight hours a week to this project, or roughly the time that a little league coach might give. If you can't give this much time, you may find techniques and pointers in this piece that will help you develop rewarding activities for young people, but a long-term attempt at the development of a troupe may very well not succeed.

You can get a show going, if that's your aim, but to keep it going, you'll have to put in some time.

Who Are Your Actors?

Another deceptively simple, but critical, question. Your criteria for admittance into a youth theatre program will greatly influence the outcome of your work. If your school has an existing drama program, you may find that you are instantly besieged, upon announcement of your workshops, by "theatre kids," who will proceed to dive into the work wholeheartedly. There is certainly nothing wrong with this. However, if you think back to the little dialogue at the beginning of this book between teacher and principal, you'll remember that most theatre students in secondary education aren't students at all: they are thrust into roles in scripted plays without a bit of training. As a result, these eager beavers may come loaded with a set of bad habits that will actually make your job harder. However, with your good training, some of these kids may stop *performing* and start *acting* in short order.

It also may be the case that in your work you are interacting often with student leaders, members of the student senate, and so on, whom you naturally wish to include in your program. But it is perhaps most effective to adopt a liberal open-door policy and encourage young people from widely diverse backgrounds and cliques to take part in your workshops. Often the kids who are actively solicited by well-intentioned adults to join a group of this nature are already the superstars of the high school, and they don't have the time or the need for such a program. The youth theatre group might attract kids who are not into sports, student senate, or academics. If you are averse to these oddballs, as some teachers will readily admit they are, then do everyone a favor: volunteer for and support one of the more conventional after-school activities. It is most likely that the kids who want to make a youth theatre troupe need a leader who is comfortable with them in their oddballness.

Having fired this shot across the bow, the following paragraph is more for nonteachers who might be contemplating an after-school or out-of-school program, as teachers already know this information.

Within most high schools a number of definite groups will exist. Three of the most commonly found are the "jocks," the "burnouts/ freaks/stoners" (this group is always identifiable, but the name seems to vary widely from school to school and year to year), and the "preps." Theatre can become a common denominator for the natural actors within each of these groups and the kids who belong to no group. However, the kids themselves may be wary of each other, as peer pressure and otherness is a powerful force in high school. Fortunately, theatre is an almost magical tool for getting people past their own inherent prejudices. If you succeed in attracting a blend of creative kids from diverse youth subcultures, you will be on your way to building a truly unique and powerful program.

It is probably best, in your initial outreach attempts, to keep it simple. State your objectives plainly. I have seen a number of embarrassingly named efforts aimed at youth outreach, devised by adults who attempted to fathom the hip jargon du jour. In fact, the previous paragraph citing the "jocks," "burnouts," and "preps" makes me shudder. By the time this book hits the printing press, chances are those kid-generated group names will be hopelessly obsolete, and as an adult, I may be unaware of this fact. I strongly urge you, don't succumb to this desire to be hip in your outreach attempts. Just tell the kids what you're trying to start in simple, plain English. Then, let *them* name the group. Over the years, I have directed of a number of student-named groups, including the Northway Construction Company, the In-Lieu of Detention Theatre Company, and the Spaha Performance Group. Each of these groups became a group partly by finding their own name together. How I shudder to think of the outcome if the Northway Construction group had been solicited to join the Super Stars! that one human services colleague suggested! (This group was funded by a program with the acronym SSTARS.)

Theatre isn't for every student. The expectation that some students will not find the process to their liking, and will quickly drop out, is a highly reasonable one. An attempt to keep a student interested through an initial period of hesitation is reasonable; an attempt to coerce a student into continued attendance through authoritarian means is not. Experience has shown that this latter approach will not succeed. Even in a program at Greene Correctional Facility, the inmate-writer-actors were all volunteers, and often, when their habitual prisoner-resistant/passive-aggressive behaviors hampered the process, merely reminding them that they had the choice of leaving the program at any time worked to restore the group. Of course this was a *weighted* choice, as the group offered respite from the brutality of day-to-day prison life, as well as an extra cup of coffee per day.

If your work is in the prevention field, then you may be completely comfortable working with the underachievers, the challenged, the oddballs, the "at risk"; in fact, this may be your goal. If so, great. But beware: such terms as *at-risk* and *high-risk* set groups apart from each other as surely as the terms *retard* and *nigger*. You may find, particularly when dealing with funding sources, that you must use these terms (*at-risk*, not *retard*) in writing. In the spoken realm, consider simply referring to the young people you work with as "the company," "company members," and so on and let it go at that. It is inevitable that you will end up using the word *kids*, which some view as pejorative. Maybe it is, maybe not. There are worse things one can be called. It so happens that I am a myopic recovering alcoholic with a physical disability and sleep apnea; my income is closer to the poverty level than I would like. This would, presumably, allow others to bestow the label "high-risk adult" on me. Now, I will admit I've been called worse, but who would appreciate that label? The problem of stigmatization of youths from high-risk environments is known to the greater prevention community (OSAP 1990b, 41).

Along this general train of thought, you may end up in a quandary over accepting or rejecting a student who is doing poor or marginal academic work. Worse, you may be in a system that demands that you reject such a student. More tools for your use in advocating for such a kid: students have often improved their school work during involvement in such a program. I have seen students who were dropouts resume study, and students with severe attendance problems redouble and recommit their efforts toward the educational process because of their involvement in a troupe. I knew one young man who, although very bright, had been put into a BOCES (Board of Cooperative Educational Services) cooking program by his high school, who found through his newfound love of theatre that college was something he wanted. That student, against all odds, went on to college, majoring in theatre. Today he lives in New York and is a working professional in costume design. In the aforementioned program at Greene Correctional Facility, a playwriting program sponsored by the Kennedy Center's Very Special Arts program, inmates were seen to have reading levels improve by as much as *four grades* during the course of a six-month program!

Dramatis Personae

OK, so you get a group, and it's got some of the square pegs, shall we say. There are a few recognizable types you are likely to encounter.

Jimmy Dean, Jimmy Dean   He just wants to hang out in the workshops. He's quiet, perhaps shy, perhaps blatantly antiestablishment. As long as he doesn't disrupt the process, he should be encouraged to continue attending. Often these quiet ones develop and become vocal and responsible members of the troupe. In all your work in this area, try to maintain an attitude of gentleness and patience. Sometimes all a young person needs is to be told that he is important to the group, whereupon he *becomes* important to the group. This holds true for the following type as well.

Norma Jean, Norma Jean   She's blonde, she's pretty, she's desperately interested in being on stage, and she will do *anything* and *everything* to prevent her real personality from showing through. Puberty has provided this lost child with the biological tools needed to gain attention, and she has thrown in her lot with that one aspect of life as her entire persona. It is quite possible that she is a survivor of childhood sexual abuse; you will need to be vigilant and be willing to make appropriate referrals. In the meantime, you will find it necessary to subtly downplay her overtly sexual persona without broadcasting disapproval of her as a person. (This is hard; she doesn't know who she is. . . .) Try to praise her for her *mind*, try to avoid placing her and Jimmy Dean in a dark corner together, and give her tasks/roles she would never expect—playing the baby, playing the dog, playing the grandmother, helping with tech. Help her break through that Maybeline shell, if you can.

Norman Bates, Norman Bates   *Intense* nerd vibes, pretty smart but probably not very well rounded, Norman can tell you everything there is to know about, say, MacIntosh-tube amplifiers, but he doesn't know what a rave is. He's gay, but he hasn't even *begun* to tackle *that* issue. Here's the tough part: All the other kids hate his guts, but they can't say so, and they don't know why. As a result, they hate him, plain and simple, yet try to be nice to him. He would probably do well running lights; maybe you can get him acting with Norma Jean as the grandfather. This guy needs your program, but don't let him become your shadow, which he will want to do.

Razzmatazz! Male, maybe female, knows the score to two or three Broadway shows by heart. Willing to burst into song at the drop of a hat. Like Norma Jean, he's desperately afraid of anything approaching simple realness. Razz wants to perform, not act, and wants to be surrounded by people, but he doesn't know how to have friends. Usually a bit of a doormat, he may have a constant companion of the opposite sex who treats him as a sort of servant. Unrequited love is a big part of Razz's reality. Treat this one with gentle respect, but keep pushing the glitzy persona away from your stage work. Razz has a lot to share but a long way to go before he gets real. It may not happen in your time with Razz, but you can serve by example. There is a great pain somewhere that is being covered up by all the glitz, and you may never know exactly what that pain is. Above all, Razz needs a safe place. Make sure you provide it.

Lucy She will appoint herself stage manager and perhaps even director. Since Charlie Brown left her, Lucy has wandered the world in search of a forum for her bitchy pseudo-adult act, which is the act she has used in the past to get approval. She needs to learn to smile and to be loveable. The initial impulse will be to put her in some sort of position of authority in the group, because, with her color-coded Trapper Keeper, she's apparently more organized than you are. Don't do it. Get Lucy to play. Help her be a little girl.

Other types you'll encounter: The big overweight kid who hates everybody. The big overweight kid who *loves* everybody. The constant crisis kid who's been in therapy and wants to "process" *everything*. Five or six or seven kids with untreated ADHD, who can't, I repeat *can't*, sit still or shut up. The punk rocker who really *has* read the books he mutters about when a concept is discussed, who oozes disdain, and who craves, secretly, approval more than anything else.

And more, and on, ad infinitum. You'll get a *theatre group. Love them.* Find the way, with each of your kids, to keep pouring that love in, even when they spew it back out at you.

They will never thank you. The *work* is full of thanks.

The parent You will encounter a number of types of parents. Most will be happy their child is involved and will limit their own involvement in your program to showing up to a show, camcorder in hand. A few will be in touch with concerns or blatant mistrust; you will have the ability to soothe them with great diplomacy, of course.

If your program lasts any length of time, you will encounter "the parent with nothing better to do."

Not to be sexist, but this is usually a mom. She loves the idea of Johnny or Melissa being in a theatre troupe and wants to help. She has a poor understanding of what you are trying to accomplish, and an even poorer understanding of boundaries. She *loves* the kids, brightly assures you that they all love her, and totally misses the fact that her child is horribly embarrassed by her (constant) presence. She will brightly interrupt your teaching to contradict you, thinking she is helping. Find, if you can, the courage and tact necessary to *get this woman away from your rehearsals.* She does not belong there. She may indeed be a great help to your program, but you need to find tasks that take her away from the process and limit her contact with your troupe. If you don't, your work will be compromised. Costumes, phone calls, baking cookies, a trip to Moscow—anything to get her away from the process. You may choose to privately talk to her about the fact that it isn't really appropriate that she spend large amounts of time in your rehearsals. Do this carefully, speaking of general principles rather than the simple, specific "You drive us all crazy!" statement you wish you could scream at her. You might encourage her to find an adult community theatre group to inflict herself on.

What Are Your Resources?

Youth theatre is an extremely inexpensive and cost-effective way to reach youth, but there are some expenses. If you have access to a small startup fund, so much the better. If you don't, you will have to put some thought into acquiring funding. Later in this piece I will discuss in greater detail costs you may incur and sources of possible income. I'll also touch on the topic of fees and dues, or tuition, versus a free program.

For starters, you need

yourself, and your willingness to learn with your kids

the kids

a space to work

a few chairs or boxes to sit on

Everything else, really, is luxury. You'll find, if your group develops, that you'll want lots of other things. Stone soup is the key. You remember the old children's tale? The wanderer comes to town with a stone, which, if put in a pot and boiled, will make a delicious soup. Of course, the soup would be even better with a carrot—and so he goes through the town, gaining an onion here, a bit of parsley there, until the town sits down to a wonderful meal indeed. You, lucky person, have by starting a troupe become the keeper of the stone.

What Are Your Qualifications?

You don't necessarily have to have a lot of theatre training for this work; in fact, this book is predicated on the assumption that you quite likely don't. If you have an open, willing attitude, you're willing to experiment with the workshop outlines and ideas presented herein, you're not averse to looking into other sources than this book for additional instruction and resources, and you're willing to screw up creatively, you're the right person for the job.

The role of director is slightly different from the conventional role of teacher. The director of a youth theatre troupe must be foremost a colleague of the young people in that troupe. From the very start you need to develop the discipline of the troupe in an authoritative, but not authoritarian, fashion. Usually the first exercise with young people in a new workshop is a name game, simply a mnemonic exercise to help everyone learn all the names. By beginning the process by sitting on the floor in a circle, you will start to break the established paradigm of the student-teacher relationship.

By so doing, an openness is established that permits group creativity. Likewise, when beginning trust exercises, always be the first participant. By taking this largest risk first, you show the group that you are a member who is in charge of teaching/direction, not an authority figure who stands apart from or above the group.

This is not to say that you should be an equal, *without* authority. It is, however, to say that the teaching in this setting must be student-centered, rather than teacher-centered. You say that isn't your teaching style? Well, quite possibly you might want to skip around in this book and use some of the exercises described for warm-ups as you rehearse your drama club production of *Inherit the Wind,* or whatever. Nothing wrong with that, but this book isn't about *that* drama club.

Perhaps more important than your current level of theatrical expertise is your knowledge of resources available to young people. This means you must do your homework. If you develop a theatre piece about alcoholism, you must know where you can refer a young person who identifies problems in her own life. Bringing in qualified counselors, medical people, and so on to present factual information to the troupe, while establishing the fact that these people are available to talk to the students one-on-one, can be most helpful. More on that later.

A major foundation for all the work described in this piece is *Improvisation for the Theatre* (Spolin 1999). Buy a copy. It is the seminal work that has launched most of the improvisational theatre work in this country in the past forty years. If you haven't played theatre games in an organized workshop, it would be ideal to find a way to be a player with peers before attempting to be a leader of a youth workshop. If you can't find a workshop offered in local continuing education classes or by a community theatre, seek out an experienced player to lead an informal series of games. At the very least, get a few creative and willing friends to play with you in your living room, for several sessions, before venturing forth. Or, you might consider a summer workshop; if you are close to a major city, there is probably an improv scene nearby that includes workshops for nonactors.

This needs to be stressed: close study of the Spolin work is essential for success in this type of undertaking. (You may also reap benefits in your other duties: these games can be adapted to many interesting classroom/youth group activities.) Of particular interest is the preface—don't skip it. However, if Spolin's work were *it*, so to speak, rather than writing this I would have simply told you to buy *that* book. This book will show you how to use theatre games as your foundation, adding group process, staging techniques, and specific ideas for developing scenarios so that you can grow a real, live theatre troupe with a group of kids. Chapter 10, "Exercises," refers to specific Spolin theatre games, as well as other exercises developed by George Morrison, David Shepherd, and the author.

In addition, we will briefly look at Playback Theatre, a format of instantly dramatized personal story developed by Jonathan Fox. Fox has developed a training program in his format and can be reached through <*www.playbacknet.org*>.

You will get the most out of this book if your knowledge of theatre includes the alternative theatre. Some of the work described herein is influenced by previous work of such troupes as the San Francisco Mime Troupe, the Bread and Puppet Theatre, the Medicine Show Theatre Ensemble, the New York Street Theatre Caravan, and the Ontological-Hysterical Theatre, as well as current efforts such as Blue Man Group: Tubes and Stomp. These companies, while very different, all share a transformational, expressionist approach to theatre that is very accessible to the student actor and very effective in reaching a youthful audience. Many are descendants of the Russian agitprop theatre, which began during the 1917 revolution, its marvelous Constructivist style, and the bizarre and wonderful Futurist movement, in many ways analogous to Constructivism and agitprop, from Italy and of the same general period.

If your love of theatre comes out of your experience as an audience member, and that experience is limited to plays, predominantly American psychological realism staged on interior/box sets, then seek out the more adventurous offerings in your community. Colleges often host little-known, adventurous, alternative offerings. Whenever you go to the theatre, be prepared to jot down inexpensive and innovative techniques of staging that you can borrow.

Where Can You Work?

Assuming that you have obtained a working familiarity with Spolin's techniques, the first step is to line up a suitable workshop space. My personal experience is that even *within* a school, a "nonschool" space works best—the kids like to get away, in many cases, from the school feeling as soon as possible after the final bell rings. If you must work in a school, a standard school classroom will work in a pinch, but perhaps there is a forgotten storage room or an unused wrestling room you could co-opt. The stage of a high school auditorium is a good place, but if possible, work at first with the curtains drawn, rather than facing the yawning, empty auditorium. The intimate space then created will allow the student actors to focus on the creative work at hand, without worrying about projection. The space you choose must feel safe. That's really the bottom line.

A bit more theory: in our culture we have a picture of a theatre as a well-lit stage platform, with a sort of picture frame (the proscenium) separating it from a large auditorium, where an audience sits in the dark, passively receiving the work of the actors, who perform under the lights. This model is actually fairly new, dating back only to Wagner (the guy we can also thank for the fat lady singing). For youthful performers, it is best if we can find a more intimate performance space, and often it may be, by our choice, one where the audience and the performer can see each other clearly (not the usual case for the performer working under the lights in the Wagnerian setup common to most high school auditoriums). If your performances, when you get there, can bring performer and audience in closer contact, you will create a richer experience for both. This is one of many areas wherein your "avant-garde" youth troupe will actually be harkening back to older theatrical milieus, such as the theatre of Shakespeare.

How Do You Get Students to Come to the Workshops?

Once a space is obtained, you must schedule your initial training workshops. Two meetings of two hours' duration per week would be a good start. If your work is immediately after school, you should have some allowance for snacks, perhaps an initial ten minutes when you allow snacks to be eaten while the group assembles. This is not to be taken lightly: adolescents need to eat a lot!

Recruitment can be accomplished through announcements, fliers, and so on. A usually less successful approach, but one you could investigate, is soliciting direct referrals from school counseling staff and other helping professionals. In many cases a student referred by a counselor will take a "this must be Brussels sprouts" attitude, and that simply doesn't work! However, in some cases a student is indeed interested from the start but must overcome a long-term aversion to anything school-related. You must always remember that you are inviting your students to take part in an artistic process, and desire on the part of the student must be the motivating force. It would be folly to expect a high probability of success with a student mandated to work with you; theatre isn't a treatment, nor is it a behavior modification technique. (Of course, you may argue that it is both. Good for you, and I hope we can have coffee some day: nothing I say in this book is immune to debate.)

If at some point with a passive student you observe a flicker of interest, try to apply the "Hold this" theory: a reticent student may be coaxed into the process by putting him in charge of some minor detail, casually, on the spur of the moment, in hit-and-run fashion. (Say, for example, "Here, Joe. Mary has to make this sign . . . hold the end for her . . ." then *walk away!*) By giving the student no time to say no, you involve him in the process in a nonthreatening, no-risk fashion that opens the door for further involvement. By walking away, you remove your own control of the outcome of this gambit, which may be exactly what the student needs.

How Do You Begin Training?

The initial sessions demand no equipment other than a few chairs. Usually the actors sit on the floor as audience, using chairs only in scenes. As you develop the troupe, you may want to acquire certain basic items that will give things a more theatrical feel. See Chapter 10 for more on this.

Always bear in mind that the training should flow from low-risk exercises to high-risk ones. Begin with exercises that involve the group as a whole, rather than an individual. Then progress to working in pairs, and finally to solo work. *Never push a student into an exercise!* Make it a rule that a student may opt out of any given exercise, no questions asked. It is wise to ritually ask the question, "Has everyone who wishes to had a chance to work on this? Then let's go on." Bear in mind that the good of the group as a whole is your primary concern. The student who chronically opts out of exercises is not a threat unless the opting out is combined with disruptive behavior. In this case, try whenever possible to let peer pressure bring the disruptive student around. Only if this method fails should you allow yourself to be drawn into the role of disciplinarian.

From the very start, try to set up the program in such a way that the students realize that they are not dealing with the typical school status quo. Starting off by sitting on the floor is only one of the many cues you'll give them that this is the case. Part of this strategy involves praising, praising, praising their efforts; by high school, most verbal feedback received from teachers is in the negative, or so it would seem to many students I've talked to, who may be succumbing to the human tendency to forget praise and dwell on criticism.

Always keep the rule "let the work flow from low risk to high risk" in your mind. Consider not going into the initial work with the students with a performance date set, or indeed with a definite performance in mind. A performance should be presented to the actors as a possibility at first. If the actors are just showing up for improv, which is fun and challenging, but by its very nature demands an audience, they will naturally come to the point where they will *ask* for a performance. At this point you will have won a victory of confidence, and the process of empowering your student troupe will be well under way. If, on the other hand, the actors enter the process with a performance date looming in the near future, no script, and only a vague concept of what the piece to be developed will look like, they will be fearful and resistant.

This phenomenon of fear of freedom is not confined to high school students. The actors in one of the first of the Federal Theatre Living Newspapers were resistant. From Hallie Flanagan's introduction to *Federal Theatre Plays:*

> Every Living Newspaper has been different in history and technique, and every one has been exciting to produce. During the rehearsals of *Triple A Plowed Under* we had one night a rebellion of some of the actors who sent word by the stage manager that

they did not want to appear in this kind of performance . . . the
directors and I met with them after the rehearsal and listened to
impassioned speeches explaining why this swift, pantomimic,
monosyllabic, factual document was not drama and why no
New York audience would sit through it. . . . ([1938], 1973, ix)

Needless to say, those actors were professional adults, who had to
be calmed down by the directors and producer and coaxed back
into the rehearsal process!

Some years ago the author developed a brief Living Newspaper piece with a group of high school students in Ballston Spa,
New York. The process was, simply, wrong. Adults had viewed my
work with another troupe, process-centered work that had indeed
yielded an effective product. Despite my warnings, I was assigned
to work in a process which was crunched, that is to say that insuf-
ficient time was given for development of the piece. The performance date was set from the beginning, and because of the severe
time limitations, the entire process was a much more product-
driven one than is suggested as being wise in this piece. The student actors, predictably enough, resisted almost all aspects of the
production. Warm-ups were a waste of valuable rehearsal time.
"What's this thing going to look like anyway? How's the audience
going to know what's going on? Nobody will get it." In essence,
all of the concerns voiced by the students carried the same powerful subtext: "Don't make me look stupid out there." Taking time
to hear these concerns and begging patience, while explaining as
carefully as possible how the various production elements would
ultimately fit together, was the only possible response. As the cast
members demonstrated for themselves the potential efficacy of
the approach, tensions faded. Two of the most strident question-
ers began to see the possibility of real success and became two of
the most helpful supporters of the project.

The Ballston Spa story has a mixed happy/unhappy ending,
depending on one's point of view. Two well-received performances
went off at the high school, and the show went on the road to
three performances for a neighboring community's high school.
But the angst that was created in the student cast could have been
avoided with a lengthier, more gentle process. In addition, the performances of this troupe showed many of the benchmarks of the
amateur performance: rushed delivery of lines, unnatural pauses,

stiff body postures, and so on. Finally, the troupe was given the opportunity to perform its piece before a countywide youth theatre
conference produced by the author. Whereas two other youth theatre troupes had 100 percent attendance at the daylong conference
preceding the evening performances, with most members arriving
early, eager to help with setup, the Ballston Spa troupe had only a
few members attend the conference, and several key members of
the cast failed to show up for the performance. In a troupe where
the work is allowed to develop organically, such annoyances are
simply not seen. The real benefit of the work for the kids surely includes the bonding that makes any chance to be with the group
seem like a treat. You can't develop that bond with a fearful group.
Consider the risk you are asking a high school student in the throes
of adolescence to take by embarking too quickly on such a project!

How Do You Set the Right Tone?

It is imperative that the student actors be empowered from the
very start. Over the years I have developed a little routine wherein
I lay out to the class my role. I present this "bit" as an option,
bearing in mind that it won't suit everyone's individual teaching
style.

first class lecturette: authority

Purpose: To break the ice, begin demonstration of playful role-play,
and encourage students to consider group/authority structure

Group size: Any

Equipment: Chair, pointer, ruler, pen, piece of chalk

Source: Burns

To begin, introduce yourself. Then say: "Now, all of you don't realize it, but over the last ten or so years, you've been trained by
the school and the people in it to respond to certain cues. You see,
when you first walked into kindergarten (jump up on chair or
desk, with pointer in hand, and do a character transformation to a

large monster), you were met by someone who said, "HELLO, BOYS AND GIRLS, I AM MISS HORRENDOUS, AND I AM IN CHARGE!" (Break character.)

Continue: "That person was giving you a strong nonverbal cue that the big person with the pointer was in charge."

Jump off chair and trade the pointer for a ruler. Continue: "By second grade, the pointer was traded in for a ruler, but the message 'JOHNNY! STOP THAT THIS INSTANT!' was still the same. By sixth grade, we were down to this (pick up pen), and you knew what it meant. Now, in high school, I bet you have at least one teacher who has it down to a tiny piece of chalk." Play gum-chewing coach-who-teaches-math: "OK, peepul, we gotta lotta work ta do today, peepul, so let's settle down!"

If there is a window available, go and open it, and throw chalk away while discussing. If not, use a wastebasket. If there is no wastebasket, swallow the chalk. The calcium will build strong bones.

"In here, we have to develop the authority together—I don't want to be the person with the pointer all the time. That means that we have to have the self-imposed discipline as a group to get our work done with a minimum amount of disruption. Therefore, while I am teaching these workshops, when things get so that I can't hear or be heard, I'm just going to be quiet, and I'll ask you all to take charge and get the group in order. That way, I don't have to waste a lot of energy playing the bad-guy teacher, and you don't have to waste a lot of energy playing the bad-guy student, and we can all find out what new roles we can play."

This miniature performance accomplishes several things. For one thing, in assuming three characters plus your own narrating self, and using the chair for height, you have subtly cued the actors to think transformationally, rather than realistically or representationally.

At this point in the first class, you need to explain that because it is the first class, you need to do most of the talking, but that in future classes you won't talk so much—that in fact, the class has permission to say, "Shut up, already," if you get long-winded. When, in a subsequent class, someone tells you to shut up, get a reality check from another student ("Is he right? Am I talking too much?"). If the student agrees, go immediately into the next exercise. By giving the students this power (in a way that they would never expect a teacher to give it to them) you free up the class to take responsibility for its own pace—and invariably the "shut ups," when they come, are said lovingly and with good humor.

It is easy to imagine that by this point some readers are saying, "That would never work! I couldn't permit such a breach of my authority!" If you are one of those readers, you're right. If however, you are interested in trying something new, this is written to urge you to shake off your accustomed demeanor and attempt this approach. If it's any comfort to you, know this: you'll have to reassume your mantle of authority later on.

In fact, later in the process it will absolutely be necessary to make it clear to the group that you are transforming your role from teacher to director and must change your way of dealing with the group. Peter Brook describes this necessary change of role beautifully in *The Empty Space:*

> There is another point the director must sense. He must sense the time when a group of actors intoxicated by their own talent and the excitement of the work loses sight of the play. Suddenly one morning the work must change: the result must become all important. Jokes and embroideries are then ruthlessly pared away and all the attention put on to the function of the evening, on the narrating, the presenting, the technique, the audibility, the communicating to the audience. So it is foolish for a director to take a doctrinaire view; either talking technical language about pace, volume, etc.—or avoiding one because it is inartistic. It is woefully easy for a director to get stuck in a method. There comes a moment when talk about speed, precision, diction is all that counts. "Speed up," "get on with it," "it's boring," "vary the pace," "for Christ's sake" is then the patter, yet a week before such old timer talk would have stultified all creativity. (1968, 126)

How does this authoritarian approach jibe with the "first among equals" role for the director that has been thus far described? Further, didn't we establish that the focus must be on process rather than product? What gives here? Quite simply, *at the right time,* such authoritarianism *is* good process. Brook points out that "a week before such old timer talk would have stultified all creativity." In other words, this authoritarian aspect of the director's role must come into the process late, rather than early. In order to get a group to start truly improvising, it is necessary to introduce a sense of playfulness and freedom that is lacking in many typical school situations. The student actors must relearn how to color outside the lines, how to make a hat out of the brown paper toweling and paste that is "supposed" to be for another purpose. Once that freedom and playfulness exist, *then* the reinforcement of strong discipline, with the goal of performance in mind, will forge a new and mature relationship between you and the student actors. They will grant you power in support of your common goal, rather than sullenly accepting your power because you carry the stick.

The ideal relationship between you and your students in this enterprise is described by Daniel J. Levinson in *The Seasons of a Man's Life:*

> What are the various functions of the mentor? He may act as a teacher to enhance the young man's skills and intellectual development. Serving as *sponsor,* he may use his influence to facilitate the young man's entry and advancement. He may be a *host and guide,* welcoming the initiate into a new occupational and social world and acquainting him with its values, customs, resources and casts of characters. Through his own virtues, achievements and way of living, the mentor may be an *exemplar* that the protege can admire and seek to emulate. He may provide *counsel* and moral support in time of stress.
>
> The mentor has another function, and this is developmentally the most crucial one: to support and facilitate the *realization of the Dream.* . . . (1978, 98)

In our case, the dream is performance.

What Should You Teach First?

At your first meeting the students should begin the important work of being on stage. After as brief as possible a time spent outlining goals of the workshops and minor housekeeping details, you should introduce Spolin's exercise Exposure (1999, 51). Following that, you should begin a discussion of the three basic building

2   Where and Beyond

polin establishes three very important concepts we need to discuss: the Where, or the physical world the scene portrays; the
What, or the physical activity engaged in by the characters; and
the Who, or the relationship between the characters. For example:
Where: Kitchen, middle-class home in Brooklyn. What: Coming
home, mending stockings. Who: Husband and wife. Arthur Miller
(1949) used these rather pedestrian frameworks well in *Death of a
Salesman*, so fear not the mundane: it is a rich vein indeed.

Where, and space work in general, is the backbone of successful improvisational technique, and in the early classes you should
spend what might appear to be a disproportionate amount of time
on Where and space work. However, a backbone without muscle
isn't worth much, unless you're a taxidermist, so you must also
quickly instruct your student actors, experientially of course, in
the process of transformation. The transformational process is
best introduced at the close of day one, when you teach the group
the beginning of the group warm-up. Leave the Who (relationship) work until later in the process. Reason: the Who is the most
natural instinct of the early improvisor, and the most apt to get
the actor bogged down in a scene. Effective theatre developed by
young people is more apt to result from a group that is very well

rounded in Where, What, and transformational techniques than it is from a group that is well grounded primarily in the factual content of the piece and that relies on stereotypical character work in the construction of the piece.

Particularly if we examine a piece about alcoholism, but also in many other instances, the information will be dry and uninteresting, or veer dangerously toward the psychodramatic modality, unless the group possesses the ability to imagine its application in an unusual, insightful, and disciplined fashion. Strong technique will give the students the freedom to get beyond their initial natural resistance and fears of the topic material, while preventing them from falling into uncontrolled reliving of traumatic life experiences.

For example: In giving the first object exercises (Spolin games that teach the actors to handle imaginary objects), there is, in some high school groups, a probability of 90-plus percent that one of the first objects shown will be a joint or a pipe. It is critical that when this occurs, you sidecoach (Spolin's term for speaking to the actor while the exercise is in process) only about the objective work being performed: "Can you feel the temperature? How about the texture? Allow it to take up space in your hand. Show us the smoke as it gets in your eye!" You may have a strong anti-pot-smoking reaction (and/or you may be as amused as the majority of the class), but your task is to focus on the work, *not* to make editorial comments. In this way you will develop the group into a safe place where controversial topics can be dramatized without fear of censorship, and the focus is on clear showing of reality, rather than "should" messages, which inhibit growth and creative inquiry. In the process you will be taking a large step toward developing the group's trust of you as human being. If you must veer away from the joint, for your own comfort level, you can, after focusing on the reality of the object, introduce on the spot the exercise Transforming the Object (Spolin 1999, 195). However, be forewarned: a joint may become an even more sinister object if the student actor senses your hidden agenda and decides to engage in testing behavior! Better, perhaps, to wait until a feedback period, when you can honestly share you discomfort at seeing the joint portrayed. The scenario might go something like this:

Teacher: Your space work improved during the exercise, we've certainly agreed on that. I had a hard time focusing: I hate what I've seen drug use do to people I know, and what it does to lots of kids and families, so I had a reaction to your choice of object. But the space work, as I said, got more specific. Problem with a joint, though: it has little weight. Maybe next time think about something really heavy to work with?

Student: Like a big ol' bong? (*One or two laugh, the rest of the group is quiet.*)

Teacher: If you're in a scene where you need to show a bong, fine. But do you think you're able to show us somebody fixing a car?

Note the subtle challenge to the difficult student's ability—it isn't accidental. Difficult students are often the best actors. Predictable reactions to the initial exercises will pass, and the more exciting work will soon begin.

Initial work with a group falls into three general areas: improvisational training, training in group process, and factual instruction on the topic at hand. This initial work is followed by the stages of development of a theatre piece, which starts to grow naturally out of the synthesis of these three areas. The training in improvisation is lively and fun and of course you will want to start there, but at the same time you will begin laying the groundwork for training in group process very early by stressing the empowerment of the group, and the ability of the individual to control her involvement. Some of the more advanced Spolin exercises are wonderful jumping-off points for discussions and demonstrations of functional group communication; try to let the work lead you to the logical starting point for that aspect of the training.

At the start of the process, spend just a few minutes each class presenting factual material about the subject of the piece to be developed. It may be the case, as in a grant-funded program, that it is necessary to administer pre- and post-testing of the group's knowledge of the subject to be covered. If this is necessary, such a test can be presented in the context of the work to be developed, reminding the actors that anything they don't know at the first taking of the test will be useful to identify, because it is probably something the audience won't know either. This focus on the work, and making a conscious bow to the permissibility of getting an answer "wrong," frees the actors from any test anxiety they might have. Following up on this through the process, you will present or go over a few factual questions in each session. Literally two or three facts per class, delivered in such a way that the actors can comment and discuss, suffices early on. As the work progresses, increased amounts of information can be brought in to a given class. Later, in Chapter 7, I will describe some possible shapes for scenarios and ways they may be developed.

Brief mention has been made of publicizing your workshops with fliers and announcements. You should shoot for an initial group of about twenty students. There will be a natural attrition process that will leave you with about a dozen core members. If that attrition rate seems high, consider that many students will be initially curious but find the actual process to be not what they expected, or scary, or what have you. You may also find that some who are interested have other commitments that pop up, such as jobs or sports, that prevent their regular attendance. Again, I have always had great success with a liberal open-door policy—a student may wander away for weeks but come back in when a performance nears. Encouraging such a student to find a small part in the production may be doing him a great service.

Let's take a closer look at the structure of your first workshop, which will set the tone for all that is to follow.

If the workshop is to begin at 3:00, *begin* at 3:00, even if there are only two students present. The ten who arrive at 3:05 will get the message. After a brief introduction of yourself, outline your initial goals: to introduce the students to improv, to have fun, and so on. Then mention your *possible* secondary goal: to develop a topic-specific piece. It is now 3:05 and that late group is wandering in. Get everyone in a circle (assuming you don't know names) and play a name game. If you already know names, play Kitty Wants a Corner (Spolin 1999, 408) followed by Who Started the Motion? (Spolin 1999, 68).

Plan: Initial Workshop

1. Introduction
2. Playback Name Game
3. Kitty Wants a Corner
4. Who Started the Motion?

5. Three-Game Warm-Up: Mirror, Rebound!, Space Rebound!
6. Transforming the Motion
7. Part of a Whole
8. Introduction of Who, What, Where
9. Exposure
10. First Object Exercise: Soap
11. Conclusion

Introduction

Have all students sit in a circle on the floor while you introduce yourself and the purpose of your workshop, *briefly.* Welcome everyone. Go right into warm-up.

playback name game

Purpose: To break the ice, connect students with vocal expression

Group size: Up to twenty

Equipment: None

Source: Jonathan Fox

Get the group standing in a circle. Watch out for a "cracked egg" formation, but also make sure players have enough room to swing their arms without hitting each other. Explain: "In this game, you are going to say your name the way you feel right now. Everyone then immediately plays it back for you, just the way you said it. Everyone around the circle in like fashion. I'll go first—(say name)—now everyone play it back, just the way I said it . . . great!" Remember: you take risks first! If you are feeling scared, express it with your name. Also, please be willing to see this exercise yield incredibly unresponsive results; these kids may be scared, and do not wish to look foolish. Praise mediocre commitment and show that you are *delighted* with anything more than that.

kitty wants a corner

Purpose: To energize the group and develop sensory awareness

Group size: Up to twenty

Equipment: None

Source: Spolin (1999, 408), citing Boyd

For this exercise, the group stands in a circle. "It" ritually goes around, clockwise, from one to the next, saying, "Kitty wants a corner." The response is "Go ask my neighbor." The object of the game is to trade places with other group members behind It's back, initiating movement with eye contact and nods, without It successfully gaining one of the place-changer's places in the circle before they do. If It gets to the place before the would-be place-changer, that person is the next It. This game gets a group moving and freed up, but watch that it doesn't get too wild. You also should be willing to take a dive, so to speak, if there is a member who simply is too slow to get out of the It role. Usually that kid is fat, which the author was as a child. Take it from me, he or she *hates* this sort of thing.

who started the motion?

Purpose: To energize, build group nonverbal skills

Group size: Up to twenty

Equipment: None

Source: Spolin (1999, 68)

You are It first. You say: "This is a child's game called Who Started the Motion? I'm going to be It first, and (pick anyone at random) is going to be the first leader. The leader will start a simple, repetitive motion, like this (demonstrate), and everyone else will mirror it. Fairly often, as often as possible, the leader will change the motion and everyone else will, too. My job is to figure out who the leader is. Then, when I pick the leader, the leader becomes the next It, and I pick the next leader, and we go on from there. Let's try it."

Show/remind the group that the repetitive motion must be mirrored exactly and changed often. You may want to ham it up a little bit to help break the ice. Pick the wrong leader a few times before the right one, for example, to get them laughing and moving.

Note: This game is great with music! If a tape or CD player is handy, use it.

three-game warm-up

Purpose: To develop kinesthetic sense, introduce improvisation

Group size: Up to twenty

Equipment: None

Source: George Morrison

Have everyone get with a partner she doesn't know. Have two players demonstrate Mirror. Lead the group through Mirror with leader, switch the leader, then teach the Follow the Follower version of Mirror (Spolin 1999, 62).

Sidecoach "Now, let's start in neutral position; that means your feet are about shoulder width apart, hands hanging at your side, knees just slightly bent—breathe! Good. Make eye contact with your partner, and start to mirror the small motions your partner's body makes. You want to follow more than lead, although you may start some of the motions. See if you and your partner can work together to make a mirror so accurate that it really looks as though there is a reflection. Remember to keep eye contact with your partner—that's good—work together—each of you is following the other. Remember that if you find yourself leading, you are not solving the problem. The problem is to follow at least as much as you are leading. Remember to keep breathing!"

Next, have two players demonstrate Rebound! Explain: "Rebound! is an action game where a sound and motion is answered with a complementary sound and motion. You do this all the time in your own life." Demonstrate waving to neighbor with "Hi," neighbor waving back with "How are you?," "OK!," or whatever. "However, in Rebound! we repeat the exact same motion and sound over again, and repeat the response also, three or four times, like this (demonstrate with fingers). Now, please know that (act out a frustrated shrug) 'I don't know what to do!' *is* a sound and motion, so in saying that, you've solved the problem. You really can't fail at this, so give it a shot. Let's have Fletcher and Valori demonstrate. Great! Now, let's all try!"

After all have tried a sound and motion followed by a responding sound and motion, say: "Great! Now, here's the deal. That initial sound and motion is repeated, as exactly as possible, three or four times. If nothing else happened, this would be a boring game. So, after you've done a sound and motion response three or four times, player A is going to *change* his sound and motion, but player B is going to *keep on* for two or three strokes with her original sound and motion, before responding with a new stroke. See how it feels when you get that new sound and motion and respond with the same repetition you've been doing—does it change anything? Give it a try!" Encourage large, non-English sounds, and big, whole body motions.

A note on this: Rebound! and Space Rebound! were invented by George Morrison. I was George's student many years ago at SUNY College at Purchase and played Rebound! his way, as I just outlined. Over the years I found, as a trainer, that I was more comfortable having the actors *instantly* respond to their partners' change of sound and motion with a new one of their own. I was puzzled by the game inventor's reason for the persistence, for a few strokes, in the old sound and motion. I recently corresponded with George, who was kind enough to reply:

> Continuation for several strokes in Rebound creates an additional problem of testing the "fit" of the complementary movement. (See below.) This is difficult without a hands-on demonstration, but I hope this is clear . . .
>
> A–B, A–B, A–B, A–C, A–C, B–C, B–C, B–C, B–D, B–D, etc.
>
> Thus, each player must find *two* fits, not just one.

I believe (I have yet to further correspond on this) that George is alluding to what some acting teachers call *adjustments*. I will report that after years of introducing this game my way, I have, with George's explanation, resumed teaching it his way. If this abstract bit of theory leaves you cold, don't worry about it—it's a cool game.

Next, introduce Space Rebound! Explain: "Consider this room for a moment, and think of it as a giant piece of Swiss cheese. The holes in the cheese are shaped like people and furniture. Artists call this way of looking at things 'exploring the negative space.' Now, if we all move our place in the room, we change the shape of that piece of Swiss cheese, that piece of space. Let's do that—everyone move to a different spot in the room—Great! Now, in Space Rebound!, we work with a partner, and moving alternately, the way you do in checkers, each player changes the shape of this block of space that is between the players. Let's have George and Judy demonstrate for us."

Sidecoach "Great. Just move one at a time, concentrating on the shape of the space between the two of you. Wonderful. Make a new shape with each move—see the shape of that space—use your whole body." And so on.

Quickly recap "We've now learned Mirror, where we reflect each other; Rebound!, where we respond to a sound and motion with another sound and motion, repeating each three or four times and then changing them; and Space Rebound!, where we change the shape of the space between the two of us. Now, we are going to put it all together, but this time, at some point in the Space Rebound! part, I am going to call out 'Freeze!' When I do, you freeze, and quickly look at the place your partner's body and your body fill in space. When I say 'Scene!,' you have to immediate justify the position you find yourself in, in the middle of a scene, as though somebody just turned the TV on in the middle of a movie."

Note: This may take some explaining; some early students will want to stop for a story conference when you call "Scene." The idea is that they immediately are involved in the middle of an ongoing scene, within which they verbally (or otherwise) justify their physical position in space. Early explorations will feature lots of hand-to-hand combat, dance instruction, and carrying of objects. A challenge, as the group advances, is to outlaw these common choices, in search of more bizarre ones. As the group progresses, you might alter the play by calling "Freeze!" during the Mirror or Rebound! portions of the triad.

Do all three games, sidecoaching each. Then freeze into scene. Be prepared to have to yell "Space Rebound!" several times—Rebound! gets noisy. Then say: "At this point, everyone here has now made a short piece of improvisational theatre. Congratulations! Let's try it again." Run Three-Game Warm-Up once more. Don't forget to sidecoach!

tranforming the motion

Purpose: To introduce transformation

Group size: Up to twenty

Equipment: None

Source: Unknown; it *feels* like a Spolin game

Get the group back into a circle. Begin: "Now, the next game is important because it's about transformation and sharing, and those two things are basic parts of all improv. I will start, then we will continue going around the circle. What I'm going to do is make a repetitive sound and motion, kind of like in Rebound!, but I'm going to travel across the circle with it. As I travel, I am going to *allow it to transform into something else.* Note that I didn't say 'change it' into something else; I am not going to stop one and start another, I'm going to free up my mind and body, and *allow the transformation to happen.* You might think of a flower opening, as opposed to a light switch turning on. Now, when I get across, I'm going to bring it to someone, who will mirror it as exactly as possible, and when I know he has it, I'll drop back into his spot in the circle, and he'll take it across, allow it to transform, and give it to someone else, who will take it, and so on. We'll start in neutral position, then cross our arms after we've worked, so it just gets brought to someone who hasn't had a chance to work yet. Let's try it." Demonstrate.

Be prepared to repeat instructions. Sidecoach, encouraging transformation instead of stop and start. Don't actually correct anyone, saying "that's wrong," but keep stressing the transformation. Be prepared to pump energy back into the exercise—this is higher risk.

part of a whole

Purpose: To develop group transformation skills

Group size: Up to twelve

Equipment: None

Source: Spolin (1999, 73)

Now, play another sound-and-motion game. This time, one person starts a sound and motion that represents a part of an animate or inanimate moving thing. It might be a machine of some kind, or a forest, or a solar system. With a sound and motion, the player will start a part running. When someone else thinks of another sound and motion that fits with the first player's, he adds it in. Keep adding until everyone is involved.

Sidecoach "Find where you fit in the whole—move right in—don't leave a fellow actor stranded! It isn't a group mirror—add your individual, different part. Work together!" Get it moving quickly, as people can get tired doing the same thing for a long time. That completes the warm-up.

Who, What, Where

Now it's time to introduce theatre games. Say: "Today we're going to be working on theatre games, which are a series of exercises designed to be fun but also to train actors. The three important basics of improvisation that we are going to identify and work on are the Who, the What, and the Where. The Who is a relationship between two people, like father and daughter, boyfriend and girlfriend, and so on. The What is an activity, like studying, doing aerobics, sleeping, and so forth. The Where is a place, like a classroom or the lobby of a theatre, or the stage, which is the first Where we will explore."

exposure

Purpose: To develop awareness of stage reality

Group size: Up to twenty

Equipment: Chairs or rehearsal boxes

Source: Spolin (1999, 53)

Divide group into halves. Half goes "on stage," half is audience. The exercise, which is described in *Improvisation for the Theatre,* asks that each group be "on" for thirty seconds or so with *nothing to do*—the players should simply experience being onstage. Then, give each group a simple task, counting colors for thirty seconds again. Do not tell the groups the length of time they are "on." Then ask them to discuss which felt longer and other subjective impressions of the exercise.

This simple exercise is a critical one—read your Spolin!

first object exercise: soap

Purpose: To introduce space work

Group size: Any

Equipment: None

Source: Spolin (1999, 58, Group Touch Exercise #1, modified slightly)

Say: "I want everyone to close your eyes and put your hand out, palm up. Great. Now, imagine that in your hand a brand-new bar of soap is resting. It's just out of the box, hasn't been wet yet, still has a sheen to it; feel it in your hand. Sense the weight, the texture, the temperature of it in your hand. Smell it. What kind of soap is it? Does it have sharp corners like Ivory, or an oval shape? Pass it from hand to hand . . . Great. Was everyone able to imagine the piece of soap in his or her hand?" This question sets the matrix for all feedback in Spolin exercises. It does not ask if students "did it right," simply whether or not they solved the problem.

Conclusion

Depending on the time at this point, you might want to try First Class Lecturette: Authority (see p. 20), or return to nuts-and-bolts housekeeping issues, or discuss possible ideas and wants of the participants. If you have time for the latter, invariably someone will suggest doing a play. This is your chance to plant the seed for a group-developed show by talking about the possibility of such an endeavor. You will want to introduce the topic you've picked. If the topic is alcohol/substance abuse, let the group know that in case a show is developed, you will be bringing in facts about the topic. I have also unabashedly informed the group that the bringing in of facts about the topic at hand was the way I "paid the rent," which allowed me to do the work that I love. The teen actors invariably understand this concept.

Trust Exercises

You are going to develop a group that is based on mutual support and cooperation rather than competition. This group will be structured in such a way that the normal societal push toward rivalry, evident in academics, sports, and social life, is consciously discarded in favor of a strong interdependence. In order to buck the trend, you must introduce trust exercises into your work. Trust exercises should be introduced early, perhaps at the second session.

I am at my most stern and authoritarian, oddly enough, when first introducing trust work. The reason is that it must be impressed on all participants that the exercise to be undertaken demands total focus, concentration, and strict adherence to procedure, in the spirit of helpfulness. Adolescents will like the idea of playing pranks. This cannot be allowed in a trust exercise, and any tendency to do so must be immediately extinguished.

the willow in the wind

Purpose: To develop trust

Group size: Up to twelve, no fewer than eight

Equipment: None

Source: Unknown

In *The Wizard of Oz*, there is a moment when the Tin Man has been discovered and (mostly) oiled by Dorothy and the Scarecrow. He is, however, still rusted to the ground, for his feet have not been oiled yet. He lists to one side, and is gently righted, then to the other, his entire body stiffly swaying back and forth as Dorothy and the Scarecrow keep him from falling. This basic movement is the crux of the Willow in the Wind.

Have the group form a tight circle, standing shoulder to shoulder. Make sure the students stand with one foot back, so that their legs can best support weight from the front without their bodies being pushed back. The group members hold their hands with palms out in front, at chest level, and the "truster" (you should be the first) stands in the center. The truster folds hands over chest, holds body rigid, and gives his or her center of gravity to the group. The group is to gently return the truster to center. The truster's eyes should be closed.

This exercise demands a rigid protocol. First of all, the group must remain silent: any talking is actually a physical danger. Secondly, the group must simply return the person to her center of gravity, not develop a game of catch. Thirdly, someone must monitor the group from outside the circle (after you take the risk and trust first, this will be you). The monitor is responsible for side-coaching and for "watching the door," which is a critical responsibility. Finally, the supporters must not drop their hands or lessen their concentration until the truster has been told to open her eyes and take back her own center of gravity, *and she has done this*. This exercise, for some, induces a deeply relaxing, almost trance-like state. Sometimes the truster doesn't come back to center at first prompt. If the group drops its focus too soon, the truster could fall.

By "watching the door," I mean you must be the person designated to respond to sounds or other stimuli from outside the circle. It is imperative that the actors keep all their focus on the truster. The natural response, when the door opens, is to look to see who is coming into the room. Reinforce to the group that you will do this; they must maintain their focus on the exercise.

It is also imperative that the actors understand that the truster must feel at least two pairs of hands returning her weight to center at a given time—double-teaming. This is for the simple reason that one kid may not be strong enough to prevent the truster from falling.

If, as I recommend, you are the first truster, you will need to sidecoach while you give the group your weight. In my case, I am usually the largest and heaviest person in the group, so by volunteering first, I show them that they can indeed safely support anyone in the group.

As side coach, you affirm that the group must stay focused, repeating that the goal is to gently return the truster to center. You also sternly extinguish any giggling or cross talk, stopping the exersise if necessary. Most important, you coach the truster.

For some, this exercise is easy and fun. Others it can terrify. Please do not force any member to do this exercise.

Observe the truster carefully. She must cross her arms over her chest (this protects the breasts, and offers the elbows and lower arms as handy "handles" for the supporters). She also must keep the body rigid, while letting her weight be passed to the group by leaning forward, backward, or sideways. Usually, trust is tentative at first, and you will observe that the truster reserves her center of gravity, merely bending from the waist, going through the motions of giving the weight to the group. This must be gently pointed out, and you should encourage the truster to let all the weight go. In the case of a reticent but willing truster, you will see a progression, with good sidecoaching and gentle group support.

First the truster will hold her center of gravity at the waist.

Then she will hold part of her center back by flexing the thighs and knees.

Then just the knees.

Next, she will hold a bit by flexing the ankles and feet.

Finally, with luck, she will give all her weight to the group, with the feet relaxed, not taking steps forward or flexing her feet to dig in to the floor.

In the case of a student who is willing but seemingly can't let go, you might consider the following: Stand behind the student and, maintaining a good support with your hind leg, place your hands in support on his back. Have him lean back and give you his weight. It is probable that you are the most trusted, by virtue of your status as adult leader, and the student may be able to do this with you. Show him that you can hold his weight, and gently move him up and down a bit. Then have him try again with the group as a whole. Go with your gut on this: some kids won't trust you at all, and this will be a counterproductive way to go.

It may take more than one session for some students to give their entire weight to the group. Stay gentle, and praise their courage lavishly. Explain to the group that everyone is different, and for some this is a profoundly difficult exercise.

If you encounter a person who is barely able to bend at the waist, encourage the group to tighten the circle and to gently let the person feel their hands, ready to support. Gently encourage the truster to give more weight. If there remains a person who opts out, don't let the group apply peer pressure, but revisit the exercise often, and invite participation. Praise baby steps toward trusting the group lavishly!

Adolescents need touch the way plants need sunlight. If you are careful and gentle, this exercise will become a group favorite and will work wonders in terms of building your group. More trust exercises are outlined in Chapter 10.

3 Group Process

ealthy group process is critical to a successful youth theatre company. As in other aspects of the training, in attempting to develop the communication skills of the group, an experiential approach works best. A group decision works naturally as a jumping-off point.

What's in a Name?

From 1988 to 1990 I ran a youth theatre program for CAPTAIN of Shenendehowa, a youth agency in Clifton Park, New York. After an initial period of training, I approached the group with the problem of coming up with a name for their troupe. The process of picking a name for the acting troupe served beautifully as the vehicle for training the members about group communication skills.

We set a special three-hour meeting as the time to pick a name for the troupe. I told the student actors that the process would be time-consuming, and that they might not even have a name finally chosen at the end of the three hours, that they might have to go into extra time before the process was complete.

Using the standard facilitator's easel and newsprint, I began the process with an explanation of brainstorming. I cited the name of an existing theatre group, Mabou Mines, to illustrate that a name for a troupe needn't have any logic, that it can simply be a name. On the other hand, a group such as the Moscow Art Theatre chose a name that factually summed up the nature of the group. Names can be capricious, arbitrary, or functional.

The brainstorm that ensued yielded a wide assortment of names, from the conservative the Clifton Park Youth Theatre Group to the sublime Sauteed Raspberries. When well over thirty names had been generated, I presented a model for group decision making that incorporated three possible modes: "might makes right," "majority rule," and "consensus" (these are my names; they may be called other things in other texts).

Might makes right (executive-power decision making) also served as a way to introduce hidden agendas. I told the group about the concept of hidden power, and a lively discussion of possible ways that a group could be swayed by the hidden power of a member or members ensued. Two Spolin (1999) exercises, different but closely related, were introduced and played at this point to good advantage: Hidden Problem (202) and Hidden Conflict (231).

The process of teaching a group to make a decision is much like little wooden Russian dolls, one nested inside the other inside the other. First the group had to decide what was to be decided (might makes right—as leader, the director declared that it was time to name the troupe and incidentally learn about decision making). Then, the group had to decide on a time to meet (could be mistaken for group consensus, but actually was hidden might makes right, because the director had exerted pressure on two group members to change their schedules so they could come to the meeting; this was important to acknowledge to the group as an example of that kind of transaction). Then, the group had to decide how they were going to reach a decision regarding the name, and finally, they had to decide on the name.

This chain of decisions-within-decisions served as a model for the group's growing knowledge of process. They expected, and were comfortable with, the director's executive decision in calling the group together, then were accepting, but chafing somewhat, at the process of choosing an unusual time for the long meeting; however, they became aware that this chafing was a natural consequence of a hidden-power form of decision making. The group then used majority rule to decide that they would choose the name for the group by consensus—and came achingly close to true consensus, only to reach the consensus that majority rule would be the necessary format for the final name decision. They conceded defeat after a process almost as arduous as this paragraph!

In so exploring an ideal, group consensus, several of the group members spontaneously came to the realization that the size of the group (twenty-three students) was a limiting factor in its ability to achieve true consensus. In gaining this knowledge of the limitations of a "large small group," the members were discovering a great deal about ensemble theatre in general.

The name chosen, the Northway Construction Company, reflected several things about the community—a bedroom suburb straddling a superhighway, where construction of developments and malls seems unceasing—as well as indicating an offbeat, improvisational group as opposed to a typical drama club.

Another group, the In-Lieu of Detention Theatre Company of Mechanicville, New York, basically refused to buy in to the concept of a long training session to pick a name, and came up with its name by actual consensus, after a mere fifteen minutes of brainstorming and discussion. Mechanicville and Clifton Park are only a few miles from each other but are as different as Scarsdale and the Lower East Side. The Mechanicville kids were very creative, bright kids in a blue-collar community, who identified themselves as "the bad kids," and were simply not interested in the mumbo jumbo of communication theory. As groups, the Mechanicville and Clifton Park kids had a primary difference regarding authority, which affected their process. The Mechanicville (they called it "Mickyville") kids were fast, highly irreverent, and had little time for theory. Mickyville kids were *happy* with negative attention; Clifton Park kids were slaves to adult approval. A third group, at the Charlton School, a residential facility for girls, just can't seem to get it together to name their group. In this case, the level of functioning of the individuals is too low and the institutional constraints are too high to expect a functioning group decision-making process; these girls need much more executive support from their teacher. Each group, however, has marked similarities.

This short work cannot be a complete guide to training a group in effective communication techniques. There are many excellent books on the subject available. But you can start building a functional group with the following tips.

Manage Discussion Effectively with a Minimum of Moderation

This isn't easy. A talking stick sometimes works. A talking stick is passed from person to person. Only the person holding the stick may speak. One group determined that an actual stick was not necessary; speakers verbally "passed the stick" to each other on request.

Distinguish Between Feelings, Thoughts, and Opinions

Many adults have a hard time with this. Feelings can be (over)-simplified into seven basic emotions: glad, sad, mad, lonely, scared, hurt, and embarrassed. Thoughts are cerebral, often questions, part of the logical/analytical processes of the mind. Opinions are based on the two previous components and represent a synthesis of the two. Often we say "I feel" when we mean either "I think" or "It is my opinion that. . . ." Training a group to make these distinctions, while perhaps a tiresome process for the group at first, can immeasurably aid in the group's efficiency over the long haul. This distinction is also central to the acting work, as we will learn in later sessions.

Identify Fantasy in Communication

Sometimes called "projection," fantasy is the mental process that we all go through when we decide that someone is mad at us, for example, because she appears quiet and withdrawn. We may be right, but maybe she has a toothache! Unless we check with the person, we can't be sure. Identification of fantasy and the ability to get a reality check from the other person can prevent sloppy process. This also becomes central to the acting exercises.

Identify a Clear Agenda and Stick with It

Challenge possible hidden agendas through the aforementioned process of identifying fantasy and checking. Be able to detect wandering away from the clear agenda into side issues. Be able, also, to drop an agenda in favor of a new one, if the group is truly headed in an unexpected, yet positive, direction. (This gives compulsive lesson planners the heebie-jeebies.)

Use "I" Statements in Communication

"I think," "I feel," "It is my opinion that" can save a group much resentment and resistance. "I" statements are tricky beasts—it's easy to mask a "you" statement within the framework of an "I" statement; for example, "I get really frustrated when you are so stupid."

Employ Brainstorming and Know the Ground Rules

The following ground rules for brainstorming are taken from *Joining Together: Group Theory and Group Skills*, by David W. Johnson and Frank P. Johnson:

1. All criticism of ideas is ruled out. Ideas are simply placed before the group.

2. Wild ideas are expected in the spontaneity that evolves when the group suspends judgment. Practical considerations are not important at this point. The session is to be freewheeling.

3. The quantity of ideas counts, not their quality. All ideas should be expressed, and none screened out by any individual. A great number of ideas will increase the likelihood of the group discovering good ones.

4. Build on the ideas of other members where possible. Pool your creativity. Everyone should be free to build on ideas and to make interesting combinations from the various suggestions.

5. Focus on a single problem or issue. Don't skip around to various problems or try to brainstorm a complex, multiple problem.

6. Promote a congenial, relaxed, cooperative atmosphere.

7. Make sure that all members, no matter how shy and reluctant to contribute, get their ideas heard.

8. Record all ideas. (1982, 272–73)

The second step in a brainstorming process is to have the group critically examine generated ideas. Most will immediately be rejected. But in most cases several ideas will be worthy of serious consideration, and one or more will solve the problem at hand nicely. Brainstorming is particularly important as a skill because the group will eventually be scenarizing theatre pieces and must be comfortable with the process if creative and viable structures are to be developed. In addition, more generic group dilemmas ("What should we do for a year-end celebration?") can be effectively tackled with this technique.

Employ Feedback

Your example will begin building the group's skill at giving and receiving feedback. It is critical that you consistently demonstrate this technique, to aid both in the development of the group's skill and in the establishment of a safe, nonjudgmental place where creativity is possible. In the case of Spolin exercises, it will often be noted that a given attempt to solve a problem was fascinating, but that the problem was not solved. Providing nonjudgmental focus on the problem, while noting other problems that may incidentally have been solved, will help the student actors realize that failure is a necessary and beneficial part of the creative process and should actually be encouraged rather than avoided.

Again, please bear in mind that there is a lot to this subject, and if you are unfamiliar with group communication in general, you should seek additional information before training your group. That said, here are some characteristics of useful feedback.

1. Describe, rather than evaluate: Your students will hear a statement that begins "I wasn't clear whether it was a cup or a bowl" better than they will hear "I didn't like the space work."

2. Good feedback is specific. "You hogged the scene" will engender defensiveness in the receiver, whereas "Several times I couldn't hear the end of Lucy's statements because you replied before she finished speaking" is a statement of fact, which is easier to accept.

3. Good feedback benefits both the giver and the receiver. If a student is giving feedback that is designed to glorify the giver's technique by pointing out deficiencies of the recipient, everyone loses. An example of feedback that might be sensitive to the recipient and help the giver: "Terry, I saw the height of your table move during the scene—it reminded me of the trouble I've had with table heights. Your door, though, was absolutely clear, and the knob appeared to me to be at the same place each time you used it. I imagined you were using your body as a mark for where the doorknob was in space, but didn't have a similar referent for the table—could that be right?"

4. Feedback should be directed toward improvement, not hopeless cases. In this kind of work, you will find gifted students, but you will also work with less talented kids. In cases with less talented players, it will do you no good to give feedback about nuances that you might give to some of the more able players. Tailor the feedback to the recipient. What can you find that worked, which you can reinforce, and what can you mention objectively that can be improved by this individual?

5. It's best if feedback is requested about specific areas. For example, a player who is trying to focus on more specific space work can benefit greatly by asking for feedback on that one part of her

work, rather than hearing a general discussion of all aspects of her work in the exercise. This reflects the student's readiness to learn.

6. Feedback is best given immediately. Spolin-style sidecoaching allows you, as teacher, to call out immediate observations or suggestions as issues occur. Later, as a show develops, you will probably choose to delay feedback until the end of the rehearsal, during traditional director's notes time. Delaying longer than that is less useful. Finally, there are times when no feedback is helpful, such as during an actual performance.

7. Feedback is a two-way street. Checking that the recipient understood what was said, perhaps by asking them to paraphrase it, is important. This paraphrase should be to clarify, not to signify agreement or disagreement, which is a separate part of the process.

8. Validation of feedback by others is important. If one student saw no clear space work, was this the experience of others? An objective summation by you, the teacher, might help, such as "OK, so it looks like eight out of twelve of your audience members saw the cup, but four people were unclear."

Note that reflective listening is a critical element of feedback. For more on feedback specific to the training of improvisational actors, see Spolin (1999) Chapter 2, "Workshop Procedures."

Assign Responsibility for Specific Tasks
You might very well have a functional group if that group can make a decision. If you never decide anything, your group isn't functional. Once a plan has been laid out, you can assign responsibility.

An unhealthy youth theatre group unconsciously slides into a "star system." Favoritism on the part of the director tends to create rivalries and ill feelings that can kill the ensemble very quickly. A well-functioning improv group will become a group of equal generalists, each of whom has a specialty. Encourage members to find their own niche. One student may be gifted at coming up with sound effects and transformational moments, for example, while another may be a budding secretary/dramaturg. A third may be especially good at organizing/packing props, and so on. Nonjudgmental experimentation on your part will help the student actors identify their strengths and weaknesses and stimulate the growth of a stronger company. All labor is honorable, and the student actors should learn reverence for the "lowliest" of tasks necessary to make the show happen. Theatre tradition holds that the most important person in the theatre may well be the one who sweeps the stage, especially if there is a nail on that floor!

Again, this short work cannot possibly cover all the techniques necessary to develop a functional and creative group process. It may be wise, if you feel less than up to this aspect of the work, to seek out a trainer for a one- or two-session training for the group and yourself. You know your individual learning style best. Whatever way you do it, please note that in an endeavor that demands as much mutual respect and trust as an improvisationally developed theatre piece, group process should not be ignored.

It was once the fashion to engage groups in marathon group-process training sessions. The author believes that attempting to cram an entire new way of communicating into a group of people in the course of one huge session is not the best way to go. Despite the Northway Construction Company's success at a three-hour session, mini-lessons, blended into the routine of games, exercises, and discussions, have better served. You might introduce brainstorming to decide some small issue early on, then return to the brainstorming technique now and then, so that when a really big decision comes along, the group is comfortable with this technique. Feedback, also, should be taught through example. It is very important that you, as teacher/director, avoid adjectives when evaluating an exercise. Seek instead to focus on whether or not the students solved the given problem. So, rather than "Hey! That was great!" you might say, "OK, I saw the room, I saw the couch, I believe the relationship was clear—mother and son. I thought I saw a small object in your hand, Fletcher, that was giving you some trouble, but I couldn't make out what it was."

Being this objective demands that you find more global ways to offer the all-important praise; I like to ritually thank each participant after feedback, with a "nice work! Thank you!" or words to that effect. What I am trying to praise is the *involvement*, not the product.

I ritually repeat, in early training, that it is the *attempt* to solve the problem, not necessarily the *correct solution*, which produces good theatre. This is a difficult concept for most students. They are conditioned to seeking the approval of the teacher. Some students will be made quite uncomfortable if your approval is not the arbiter of success.

If a group watches a theatre game exercise where, for instance, the actor is trying to show someone sorting bills, the feedback may turn into a guessing game if you allow the actor to say yes or no to individuals' thoughts on what was shown. The members of the group will want to please the people who just worked, and they will want to be "right." Therefore they will modify their feedback based on the yes and no responses 'till they can blurt out the "right" answer. Feedback is not twenty questions, and in that exchange, little is learned. It's good to introduce an objective feedback protocol early on, so that the actors can hear an honest assessment of their work. It might sound like this:

Director: OK. The problem to solve was to show difficulty with a small object. John?

John: I saw something, but I wasn't sure what it was . . . I thought he was trying to open it.

Director: Maureen?

Maureen: He was trying to open a child-proof bottle.

Fletcher: He was trying to strangle a rat. Or maybe open a jar.

Director: Which one really?

Fletcher: I was just kidding. I thought he was trying to open a jar.

Jeff: I saw him opening a jar, too.

Tiffany: I was unclear. I saw him struggling with something . . .

Director: OK. So, most of your audience saw you trying to open something, a medication bottle or a jar. What was your object, and what was the difficulty?

Josh: I was trying to strangle Fletcher's rat. (*Laughter*) No, it was a jar.

Director: Of what?

Tiffany: I dunno. . . .

Director: Well, it seems you mostly succeeded in solving the problem, which was to show difficulty with an object; we all saw the difficulty. The specific object was less clear. Maybe next time, if you decide what's in the jar and how much it weighs, you'll be even closer to total solution. OK, thank you! Nice work.

◢4◣ Training Your Actors

Since a troupe is more than merely a collection of actors, your workshops must incorporate more than just traditional acting training. Each workshop, ideally, should include some acting and improv work, group development and trust work, some topic work (e.g., alcoholism and substance abuse or what have you), some exploration of low-tech/no-tech multimedia (see Chapter 6), and some work on story, plot, and structure. That's a lot, which is a reason that I prescribe a two-hour session. Some bad news: much of what you try to introduce will flop, so you need to have backup plans in mind. My personal rule of thumb is to have approximately three hours of material ready for each two-hour session, just in case. When you're new to this, this may not be possible, but after a while you'll have a lot of exercises stored in your head.

Acting is probably the reason most of your kids are in the group. They love the *idea* of acting, and know nothing at all about it. As mentioned earlier, Spolin's work is incredibly useful, and I won't try to rewrite her stuff here. Instead, let's try to arrive together at a general theory of acting from which you can apply specific exercises, by Spolin and others, with understanding. Later we'll include a list of suggested texts, for those of you who are novices or who haven't taught acting before.

Some Advice from Hamlet

Speak the speech, I pray you, as
I pronounced it to you, trippingly on the tongue:
but if you mouth it, as many of your players do,
I had as lief the town-crier spoke my lines.
Nor do not saw the air too much with your hand, thus,
but use all gently . . .

Shakespeare, Hamlet *(act 3, scene 2)*

For most amateur and student actors, "performing" is deadly. The kids who want to act are performers already, it's in their blood, so to speak. That means they are for the most part eager and willing to violate all the famous advice given by Hamlet to his players, and will "saw the air" with impunity. They will mug, ham, emote, and turn somersaults to gain audience approval. They will not want to take risks, which might lead to audience disapproval, which translates as acute embarrassment. Performing obviously is also the heart and soul of acting—*if* it is integrated with a technique that allows the actor to create reality within the stage context. To put it simply, the kids your group attracts will be a bunch of hams. They will be prone to clichéd mannerisms and styles but have no real idea of the actor's technique.

Roy G. Biv and the Seven Emotions

No, it's not a band. Many of you already know Roy: you met him in art class. When talking about pigment colors (*light* colors are different), the primaries are Red, Orange, Yellow, Green, Blue, Indigo, Violet (Roy G. Biv). These are the basic building blocks, which, with black (the presence of all of the above) and white (the absence of all of the above), make up the millions of colors that we perceive each day. But can you name the seven basic emotions? A surprisingly large number of people can't.

Here they are again: mad, glad, sad, lonely, scared, embarrassed, and hurt. These basic seven make up the palette from which all of our millions of shades of human emotion are blended. Actors need to know this, but more importantly, they need to know the following, which most actors do *not* know: *You can't play an emotion!* It simply isn't possible. What you can do, as an actor, is carry out a physical *task*, such as washing the dishes (Spolin's What) while also activating a *verb*, such as *punishing*, toward your scene partner.

Here's an acting exercise for you to do right now in your head: imagine yourself carrying out the task of washing dishes (by hand). Now, include in that scene a partner, say, a spouse, whom you wish to punish. You have no words in this scene, only the task. Can you punish your spouse with the task? You might choose to slam the much-beloved Waterford crystal about mercilessly . . . or you might simply lavish great physical care and precision on the task, while ignoring the spouse (your scene partner) completely. That'll show 'em! What you've just done is imagine yourself choosing one or another specific set of actions to accomplish a task and a verb.

So:

T = Task (washing dishes)

V = Verb (to punish)

SV = Subverbs (your choice: to *bang about* the crystal or to *work with great care and precision* while *ignoring*, a second subverb). You may have any number of subverbs in here.

R = Audience reaction

In the mathematics of acting, this yields an equation:

$$T + V + (SV * x) = R$$

Note that we haven't mentioned an emotion in here. It's *my* job, as your audience, to fantasize about your character's emotions. I see you, and I use your work, plus the work of the playwright, the lighting designer, and so on to decide that you are hurt and mad, a combination of two emotions. The way your spouse picks up the piece of cracked Waterford and dries it (task), while cradling it so very gently and reassuring it as if it's an injured child (verbs/subverbs: in this case the spouse is carrying out the verb to *shame*, using the subverbs *cradling* and *reassuring* to do so), leads me to conclude that the spouse is sad and hurt.

Fact of the matter is, you as an actor may be not at all angry; both you and the other actor may be delighted to have work, or excited about opening night. You can't deny these real emotions, so you don't try.

Acting is not temporary psychosis. If I am playing Hamlet, ruminating about "To be or not to be," I had better not be really considering suicide, or I'll likely never make it through the run! Instead, as a technician, I have set for myself a series of tasks and verbs that will show the audience a reality that will allow them to fantasize. If I and the director have chosen well, the audience reaction is of high quality and appropriate. If not, well, we've all seen that outcome.

The Alchemy of Acting

Having said this, you and your actors will then sometimes find that the actor starts to feel actual emotion as a result of playing the task and the verb. When this happens for a professional actor, it's sublime: there is nothing better than that full emotional involvement, and audiences will be enthralled. Acting, in fact, is a profession where one is delighted to find oneself beating the crap out of oneself emotionally on a regular basis, say, each night at 8:47, when *that* scene comes around. However, the professional actor knows that this emotion must be used as a tool and not allowed to run rampant.

Routinely, acting students are taught to sternly instruct the emotion thus resulting from scene work to stop once the scene in question is over. *Any felt emotion that is the result of acting work is no longer appropriate as soon as the scene is over.* It is very important for actors to develop that discipline. This is another acknowledgment of the power of psychodrama and the danger inherent in letting aftereffects of deep trauma erupt in your workshop without a competent therapist on hand. I've stressed this several times in this tome—I'm not trying to scare you, simply to encourage you not to meddle too deeply. Real emotion will erupt in your workshops and you must know when it's time to intervene and when it's best to let it flow. You've got to trust your gut on this. Another reality: you won't be perfect at this, either, so don't beat yourself up over it or let it keep you from the work.

So, back to acting theory: We have a task, a verb, and a perceived-by-the-audience emotional reality. We, as actor-technicians, have to experiment with combinations of the task and verb to find one that will make the director (who represents the audience) happy.

Most directors in the theatre don't know this. They will ask the actor to "be angrier" when they really don't know *what* they want. But, like art, they know it when they see it. So if you and your youth troupe can catch this concept, you'll be way ahead of the game.

This model is also incredibly helpful from a behavioral point of view. If you are working with a group of "difficult" or "high-risk" kids, you may see passive-aggressive or not-so-passive-aggressive behaviors, which are habitual. Getting this concept of emotion/verb/task across, then discussing with your group the fact that when you feel X emotion, you have a number of choices as to tasks and verbs to express/help you deal with that emotion can really help you cut through some old (unwanted) behaviors. In fact, this allows you to casually name a behavior or verb, relate it to an acting concept, and (in a healthy way, of course) coerce the youthful actor/rebel out of that particular behavior! It beats the hell out of assigning detention, which, if you are in an after-school program, is not an option anyway.

There is another advantage of the "task" approach, as we will see in the following section.

Get the Actors Out of Their Own Way

Look back at Hamlet's advice. All of the things that drive him nuts are the hallmarks of self-conscious acting. If you can train your troupe to get so busy on stage that they have no time as actors to step outside of themselves and watch, which is the *audience's* job, I guarantee you will make some beautiful, engaging theatre.

To return to the lingo of Psych 101, this has to do with acting being an associative skill made up of a series of cognitive tasks. (All right, Psych 101 was a long time ago, and if you're like me, you slept through the lecture that day.) An associative skill is one like driving—you don't think about it much, you just do it. A cognitive task is one wherein you are actively learning and problem solving in a way that the front of your mind, so to speak, demands full involvement. For example, as mentioned, driving is associative, unless you find yourself in an ice storm, on an unknown country road, at night. Suddenly, the radio and the kids bickering in the back seat are intolerable, and you are surely not daydreaming; you demand silence as your eyes strain to see into the darkness, and your foot dances back and forth between the accelerator and the brake in an agony of anticipation. Now, driving is cognitive! Your children, still prattling on in the back, may be shocked that you are suddenly calling for silence. In other words, you and the kids find yourself in *crisis*, which, of course, is what drama is all about!

The actor's craft is, in part, a set of skills that involve blending a series of cognitive tasks, some of which appear to the audience to be accomplished associatively, with a series of associative tasks, which appear to the audience to be cognitive. Confused? I am, and I wrote that sentence. Let's both read it over, shall we? There is meaning in there. It's art.

Your work is to train your actors to have *technique* that is associative, but that technique demands that they constantly provide themselves with cognitive tasks on stage, so that they stay out of their own way. This causes their behavior and their emotions to be real, although not psychotically, as the characters they play, but as themselves. In the best case, the audience perceives another reality, a heightened one, which is more than the sum of the parts of the actors' performance. It's quite simple. And excruciatingly difficult.

You need to train your actors to understand that at every given instant they are on stage, they must be *aware* of doing something—*never* are they simply passively waiting for their line.

So, what is this technique? How do you teach it? Great questions! Let's take a look at a possible second workshop format, and see why we are doing each activity/exercise. Bear in mind that not all of this workshop is going to directly relate to acting technique, but at this stage of the game a lot of it does.

Plan: Second Workshop Session

1. Greeting and Warm-Up: Kitty Wants a Corner and/or Who Started the Motion?
2. Zip, Zap, Zop
3. Reintroductions of Mirror, Rebound!, and the First Object Exercise

4. Space Walk Series A through D
5. Reintroduction of Space Rebound!
6. Reintroduction of the entire Three-Game Warm-Up
7. Take five
8. Emerging Where
9. Involvement in Twos
10. Yes And
11. Mini-lecture and demo: lighting and mood
12. Final circle/recap/Q & A

Greeting and Warm-Up

Re-play Kitty Wants a Corner and/or Who Started the Motion? Both of these demand what the computer folks call "multitasking." You can heighten the intensity of multitasking, an important actorial skill, by having a conversation go around the circle during Who Started the Motion? Each player, in turn, can relate "the best thing that happened to me this week" and "the worst thing that happened to me this week" while continuing to play the game. This isn't easy, be ready to pull the second task and just play the game. If, however, your group succeeds, or at least comes close to succeeding, it is great, 'cause this is a model for acting in general. They have to play Who Started the Motion?, which demands intense focus on visual cues and full kinesthetic involvement, while listening and talking about a mutually agreed-on subject—with real connection rather than rote recitation. This is a simple model for acting in general.

It never ceases to amaze me, in a directorial situation: I will ask an actor (we're talking about a trained actor in a conventional stage play, here) to move, say, four feet to the left, or right, or downstage, in a given moment in a scene. The actor in question will stare blankly at me a moment, then somewhat plaintively ask, "How do I get there?" This is an actor for whom (at that moment in rehearsal) the many cognitive tasks that make up constructing a role are overwhelming, and the simple, usually associative task of moving a few feet over becomes a seemingly overwhelming obstacle. I have witnessed this or something like it in student, amateur, *and* professional actors. Obviously the answer to the question is "Walk, dummy!" But this would be counterproductive, unless of course the actor in question is such a pain (and so brilliant) that *that* answer is, indeed, appropriate. Fascinatingly, I have never had such a response from an actor in a nonscripted development process, which I believe is a testament to the training method herein described.

The combination of "best thing/worse thing" with Who Started the Motion? will be an early introduction to shuttling, an extremely important acting skill.

A shuttle, as you know, goes back and forth from point A to point B; so, too, must the actor's awareness, in the process. Now, an early workshop is not the time to tell your actors this. Rather, it is time to try to find the way to experientially show them how to develop this skill. Later in training you will literally inform them of this process, when they already have some innate ability, thus building their knowledge, skill, and self-esteem at once. For early workshops in particular, let the theory remain our little secret, and let the kids have fun.

Next, introduce a new warm-up game: Zip, Zap, Zop.

zip, zap, zop

Purpose: To break the ice, energize, and heighten awareness

Group size: Up to twenty

Equipment: None

Source: Unknown

Make sure the group is still in a circle. First person "zips" another. This means that she makes eye contact, then with an abrupt, forceful motion, slides her right hand past her left, producing a soft clap, and ends this motion with a full straight-arm point at the person she is looking at, while saying, "Zip!" The person zipped makes eye contact with another (it may be the person who zipped him) and "zaps" her. The person zapped "zops" the next, and so on. The point is that if you are zipped, you zap; if you are zapped, you zop; and if you are zopped, you zip. Deviation from this order, zipping, zapping, or zopping without the proper arm motion, or exhibiting undue hesitation means that the person who goofed must stand outside the circle.

Following the mantra "low risk to high risk," you may choose at first not to play this elimination style and just focus on the cooperative and aerobic fun of the game. At a later date in training, you may get supercompetitive and have the eliminated players on the outside of the circle find (noncontact) ways to divert other players' attention, causing them to goof.

Reintroductions: Mirror, Rebound!, First Object Exercise

Circle games completed, reintroduce Mirror, both leader and Follow the Follower style. Also take a moment to reintroduce Rebound!, asking your players to really try to duplicate their sounds and motions exactly. Have them examine for themselves (a) what happens when their partner introduces a new stroke and they must continue with the old one and (b) how it feels when they make a new stroke of their own. This isn't time for a discussion, just ask your players to note this for themselves.

Reintroduce the First Object Exercise, starting with something other than soap, then going with just a big glop of space substance, the stuff of which all improv space props are made. I find it best to introduce space substance as a small amount of stuff in the hand, and once the actors get this, to go on to Spolin's Space Substance exercises. (I have developed over the years a bit of schtick wherein I advertise *my* glop of space substance as being directly passed down from the Chicago Compass/Second City to me, and I offer to sell a piece of it to any participant, after the workshop, for a mere twenty dollars. Only in adult workshops have I found anyone so frighteningly gullible that he or she offered the twenty. . . .)

space walk series

Purpose: To develop whole-body awareness of space

Group size: Up to twenty

Equipment: None

Source: Spolin (1999, 80–83)

In this series, the actors learn to experience the space around them as a new, separate substance, not mud, or molasses, but a new thing. They learn to move through and manipulate this magical stuff, individually and together. See Spolin for instructions.

Reintroduction: Space Rebound!

After leading them through these variations, reintroduce Space Rebound! Sidecoach the pairs, who should all be working together, to use all five senses to create the substance of the space between them, and to make it a new shape each time. Keep the focus on the shape of the space substance.

A note on Space Rebound!: Be on the lookout for your students to be creating a series of representational vignettes, as opposed to keeping the focus on the space. If you see this, sidecoach with the positive remarks ("Keep your focus on the shape of the space between you") as much as possible before (as a last resort) using negative comments ("Don't make statues or scenes—that's not for now . . .").

Reintroduction of Three-Game Warm-Up

Now, reintroduce the entire Three-Game Warm-Up, with the "freeze into scene" activity. Praise, praise, praise those actors! Since they have (to a greater or lesser extent) flipped into a scene, they are improvising, which may be something that causes anxiety for some. Three-Game with "freeze," wherein the entire room is improvising together, with no critical eyes watching, is a great way to start overcoming improv anxiety.

Take Five

By now, you're probably about forty-five or fifty minutes into your class. (Or, you're into your third workshop—remember, the time thing is flexible here.) It's a good time to take five, but make sure it is five, and not more—this aspect of discipline is important to develop from jump street.

After the break, have your group "make a stage" and an "audience," meaning that they sit in a group facing an empty part of the room, which might contain a couple of stage boxes or a chair. (Make sure there's just one chair; "two-chair role-play" is to be avoided!)

emerging where

Purpose: To build space work skills

Group size: Up to twelve

Equipment: None (chair, if needed)

Source: Spolin (1999, 90), modified by Burns

Next, introduce the Where and have them play Emerging Where. In this exercise, a player starts by establishing an object onstage. Each successive player uses already established objects, but each adds another. One interesting facet of ensuing discussion: How many of your players are able to add just one object? For example, if I open a cabinet and take out a glass, I have established two objects, and if I set that glass down, I have established three. It can be very hard to establish just one. So, did I solve the problem if I established three, when I was supposed to establish only one? This is a good opportunity for you to reinforce the concept that failure—the right kind of failure—is success in theatre games.

involvement in twos

Purpose: To develop physical agreement with other players

Group size: Two

Equipment: None

Source: Spolin (1999, 65)

In this game, two players agree on an object that involves both of them fully, as in tug-of-war. They should focus on the object and their tactile involvement with it. Now, if this yields a pair who have a markedly different way of relating to their object, for example, they have a bedspread that is obviously light and easy to manipulate for one, but heavy and unmanageable for the other, discussion/feedback can be used to introduce the all-important concept of agreement. This is particularly true if one or both students are exhibiting "performing" or hammy, laugh-getting behaviors at the expense of the problem. For example:

Teacher: Fletcher, your bedspread—was it heavy or light?
Fletcher: It was a heavy sucker. (*Class laughter.*)
Teacher: OK, and Emily, yours?
Emily: Mine wasn't heavy.

Teacher: OK, and you didn't have much trouble making the bed with yours.

Emily: No.

Teacher: But Fletcher, you did.

Fletcher: I had just washed my bedspread, and I couldn't do a thing with it. (*More laughter.*)

Teacher: OK, but weren't you supposed to be working with the same thing?

Fletcher: We were!

Teacher: But, hers was light and yours was heavy. (*Fletcher looks blank, for just a second—that's the teachable moment.*) You have a gift for physical comedy, which is exciting—we're going to have fun with that. But this exercise demands that you and your partner agree, nonverbally, on the weight, the texture, the size, and so on, of the object. So, while there is nothing at all wrong with getting a laugh, you have to try to do it with the same bedspread Emily is using! Get it?

Fletcher: I have to be in the same bed with Emily. (*More class laughter, Emily hits Fletcher over the head with imaginary pillow.*)

Teacher: In a manner of speaking, yes.

yes and

Purpose: To introduce agreement with amplification

Group size: Two

Equipment: None

Source: Unknown

For this game, have two actors get up in front of the audience. One gives a simple statement of fact, such as "I like spinach," as the first line. The duo's task is to keep up a dialogue wherein each statement is agreed to and amplified . . . "yes, and" . . . thus:

A: I like spinach.

B: Yes! You do! And you like it with butter!

A: I love it with butter! And vinegar!

B: You do indeed! You even stop in the middle of the day to get some!

A: I drop everything, just to get that spinach, even if I'm not hungry!

B: I've noticed that! It's amazing—you don't even care if it's cooked or raw!

A: Cooked, raw, it's all the same to me! I'll even eat it frozen!

And so on.

Here, the actors build an increasingly ridiculous structure, based on successive agreement and amplification. It's important to instantly flag and recall "yes buts," or worse yet "nos," so the actors can see how hard it is to break our cultural norm, which unfortunately is not agreement. This little exercise also can introduce questions in scenes.

Questions   In many cases, the semipanicked early improvisor will blurt out a question to his partner. An example might be "Why are you flapping your arms?" when, in fact, the scene partner isn't flapping her arms at all. Or it might be "What should we do now?" In either case, what the player has done is put the scene partner on the spot—doubling the partner's anxiety level and quite possibly ending, effectively, the scene. In early training, I suggest that you outlaw all types of questions in scenes.

In point of fact, questions in improv are like cholesterol: there are good questions and bad questions. A good one is related to the reality of the scene, within the flow so to speak, and does not hinder, but may actually help, the partner's fuller involvement with the Who, What, or Where. An example might be "Would you hand me the hammer?" (My wife, the English teacher, will insist that this is technically not a question, but rather an *imperative*—perhaps that's what makes it "good cholesterol.") Later in training, you can introduce this concept, after your group is out of the habit of asking bad-cholesterol, anxiety-provoking questions like "What should we do?"

Agreement, without the nettling question, is the core of good improv and may be a great place to end your second session. Discussion might also include your introduction of the importance of trust and the setting up of the next session's trust exercises. (By the way, on the subject of agreement and trust: one of my favorite Viola Spolin quotes: "Anyone who steals a scene is a thief.")

Mini-Lecture and Demo

To change the mood a bit, you might want to now throw in a mini-lecture and demo, on lighting, for example.

You will need a strong flashlight or a clamp-on scoop reflector light, some blue, pink, and yellow gel (theatrical color medium), or in its place some Easter-basket-colored cellophane, available at card and craft shops.

Have a student turn lights off, and have another student light you as follows as you speak:

from off to one side, and somewhat above, with the rose gel

from higher up, and more center, with the blue gel

from directly under your chin, with the yellow gel

Discussion can ensue on the various moods/situations these different lighting colors and positions could help create.

You have now very quickly and simply eased your group into looking at technical theatre in a very low-tech, accessible way. This discussion can easily slide into your closing activity for this session.

Final Circle/Recap/Q & A

It is excellent if you can manage the time such that your workshops end with this. It gives your group a stronger bond, puts a cap on the workshop, and may give you valuable insight, based on questions or comments you receive, about how to proceed with the group. Personally, as a teacher I tend to talk too much; if you share this tendency, try to find ways to get your students talking—and shut up, already!

⑤ Producing

U p until now we have been generally discussing some concepts central to the development of the youth theatre *ensemble*. This chapter will suggest specific activities aimed at getting your *program* up and running. You will quite likely be director, teacher, *and* producer of your youth theatre troupe. This chapter will concern itself predominantly with your role as producer.

A producer does everything that nobody else does in the process of putting on a show. The producer *produces*. Produces money, a venue, actors, set, lights, costumes, an audience, a house crew, tickets.

The producer is *the money*. (Maybe he doesn't own it, but he serves as conduit.)

The producer, according to many directors, is a *son of a bitch*.

The producer is viewed by business types as a *flaky artistic type*, and by flaky artistic types as a *stuck-in-the-mud business type*. Usually, the producer *is to blame, for anything*.

The producer must be *insane* to take on the job of being the producer.

If you are a teacher, you know that you are already a producer: you routinely produce your daily classroom miracles. You know that you must book a space and get permission to begin your after-school program with the administration. You are probably also already familiar with various time-honored in-the-school techniques of funding a group, such as bake sales and booster clubs. Please bear with me as I relate some practical considerations to others who work primarily outside the school, some of whom may be venturing into your building after school.

Infiltrating the School

The typical American high school is run on the factory school model. Regimentation and order are key. Schools tend to become somewhat closed off to the outside world, and administrators can seem aloof and wary of outside input. Arcane rituals and routines of paperwork and key usage can seem incomprehensible to the outsider. Given this, it is imperative that you develop a contact within the school who can run interference for you. A teacher or counselor is the best person to hook up with for getting permission to use spaces, arranging performances, and so on. If you try to do these things yourself, working directly with the administration, miscommunication and frustration are bound to result. If you will be working primarily after school, heed the following advice.

The Hard Way: Going It Alone

In 1987 I was hired by a local high school to direct the drama club production. I discovered that the bathrooms adjacent to the auditorium—indeed all the bathrooms—were locked after school. I had a cast and crew numbering perhaps fifty hardy souls, none of whom could eliminate unless the custodian was tracked down and the bathroom opened. (Actually this is only half-true. The boys didn't seem to mind, but took frequent strolls to the back of the building.) I requested a set of bathroom keys from the principal. A week later I requested said keys again. A few days later, the same again. I finally received keys only after bursting unannounced into the principal's office with a secretary desperately trying to deflect me, in grand movie tradition, and threatening to pee in the principal's coffee if a key was not summarily produced. Of course, it would have been a loss of face for said principal to give me the keys at the exact moment of my tantrum: I had to wait one more day, and I received a stern lecture on propriety.

If that were to occur today, in schools rocked by violence and perhaps justifiable paranoia, I am sure I would be arrested. This was not the way to get the key. At the time, I thought the principal Machiavellian. In retrospect, I realize that getting me, an outsider, a key to the bathroom, simply was outside of his jurisdiction. He was paralyzed by his system's procedures and didn't know how to do it.

The Easy Way: Ingratiating Yourself with Custodians

The critical ally that you must cultivate is the school custodian. After 3:00, the real power center in the school is not the main office, but rather a cramped room off the loading dock, behind a maze of floor buffers and broken lockers. The custodians can make or break your program. Understand that there is no good reason for these hard-working people to help you. It isn't in their job description. Walking into the school cold, you don't know who they like or who they dislike. You can be fairly certain that there has been some friction between the custodial staff and others with whom you will interact. There may be hidden resentments. You will at some point need their help, so stay diplomatic!

Custodians know a lot about schools. Get to know these guys and be consistently friendly and thankful! I don't mean *pretend* to be consistently friendly and thankful, I mean really be that way! A huge mistake made by some overeducated, unintelligent souls is to assume that the person who wields the mop (and the keys to the school) is stupid, or somehow less-than. You need to appreciate that this individual can do things you don't even know you need him to do—yet. Respect him. Doors will open for you that might otherwise literally remain locked forever. If a custodian takes a liking to you, you may have found the ally capable of giving you exactly the help you need to accomplish your goals (perhaps an "unofficial" copy of the master bathroom key).

If your agency conducts a community event in the school during the evening, make a point of bringing some of the pizza and soda down to the custodians' office and thanking them for their help! This simple expression of appreciation to some people who put up with far too much nonsense in their daily working lives may yield fruits beyond imagining.

Gathering Supportive Allies

Whether you are an expert on the topic of substance abuse/addiction, or a concerned novice, a certified teacher, or an entry-level outreach worker, consider bringing other professionals into the training process. Your program should take advantage of the broadest possible spectrum of inputs from community sources. Bringing in guest lecturers to present brief factual lessons on the topics covered by your group can break up the training process, thereby preventing boredom. More important, by introducing your actors to professionals from the human services sector of your community, you may facilitate appropriate referrals at a later time. Put yourself in the shoes of a high school girl who is uncertain about a reproductive issue: If you were a teen scared about possible pregnancy, would you feel better being referred to an unknown nurse practitioner or talking to your *friend* Bunny, who just so happens to be a nurse practitioner? Obviously the latter. If you can get helping professionals to relate to your troupe on a relaxed, first-name basis, you will be opening doors for further dialogue. In addition, you will be providing a number of positive role models and demonstrating that there are adults in the community who care about your student actors.

I have brought nurses, counselors, psychologists, recovering addict/alcoholic members of twelve-step recovery groups, and persons with AIDS into the group under the banner of information. Some of these people have taken a personal interest in the young people in the troupe and have established helping relationships with them.

Developing a broad base of community professionals who serve as advisors to your project can also serve the very pragmatic function of lessening criticism aimed at you about the content of your group's theatre pieces. If you can show that you assiduously sought out expert opinion in developing your program, you are less vulnerable to irresponsible charges from community members who get riled up over your group's presentation.

However, you must realize that strangers in the school building are suspect; notify everyone you need to notify before bringing in outside personnel. It's well worth the time it takes to write and photocopy a memo and stuff some mailboxes with it. Cover thine posterior, at all times.

One reason this is particularly important in the modern school is liability and the fear of same. You may be dealing with sensitive topics in a school that must ask parental permission to discuss basic life functions with students. It's best if your memo of notification is friendly and professional in tone, stressing the professional qualifications of your guest.

Timing of this memo is critical, too: Too early, and it will be claimed it was never received. Too late and an administrator may resent being manipulated. Remember that you *need* the administrator in case there is a backlash against the topics you are covering with your kids. I do find it better to subtly stack the deck by informing, rather than requesting permission. Don't give them a chance to say no without their seeming rude, and they will probably leave you alone. Does all this seem a bit paranoid? Work as an outsider in a school for a while and get back to me on that.

Do not assume that any subject is exempt from community backlash. I have been accused of "exposing our children to propaganda" after we presented a piece suggesting that mixed messages from adults regarding the use of alcohol could contribute to youth addiction/abuse. If your young troupe develops effective and powerful pieces, some of the more defensive members of the adult community who may be avoiding their own issues are very likely to take offense.

Whether you are working within a school or a community agency, your job as producer includes spin doctor. A presentation by your kids in a youth agency activity room about teen pregnancy must of course relate to the facts of how teens get pregnant, and you will face people who don't want to know that their sixteen-year-old is aware of the existence of sex. Diplomacy is key here. Pointing out to the parent that the average youth-oriented network TV show is five times more explicit than your program—even pointing it out in the least confrontational way—will only come across as defensive, bitchy, and unreasonable to this particular parent. Better yet is to modify the technique prescribed for Opie, the oppositional student (see Chapter 9), and seek assistance from someone in charge of your performance venue.

A great fund-raiser is the time-honored Halloween haunted house; your kids will be naturals at putting such an event together. But there are those who consider such activity, no matter how innocent and noble your intent, to be satanic, and they *will* confront you. Congratulations on becoming a producer! Having community/school partners who are willing and able to take some of this flack is a precious resource. Know and cultivate your allies.

Another very important reason for eliciting a broad base of support from community and school has to do with funding. If you can show potential funding sources that you are cooperating with and utilizing existing resources effectively, you stand a better chance of receiving support.

There are two general rules that may apply to almost all theatrical endeavors.

1. There is never enough time.
2. There is never enough money.

However, funding your youth theatre program may be easier than you think. Youth theatre is a highly fundable program. It is probable that you already have some resources; you presumably have a salary, albeit hardly a princely one, hopefully paid through a stable funding source. But it is also probable that there won't be money to cover everything that is needed to run your program.

You might consult local businesses about donations to underwrite parts of your program, after the fashion of sponsorship of a sports team. Canvassing group members for connections to local businesses could prove to be a gold mine. However, before you do, you need to know what you have and what you need.

Keeping a Simple Budget

Before you gloss over this part, thinking to yourself that you aren't in charge of the money (if indeed you are so fortunate), take a moment to consider that, in fact, you are in charge of *all* resources for your program, including your own energy. A budget is a very important aspect of your program. By putting down costs on paper, you can get a real and valuable idea of the strengths, weaknesses, and possibilities of your program.

A budget is a two-sided document. It must list all assets on one side and all liabilities on the other. In most budgets, these assets and liabilities, when compared, should cancel each other out, so that the bottom line is zero. You need to know that your time is money, as are material goods donated by school or agency sources. You may be shocked, if you are unfamiliar with budgets, to discover the true cost of your simple little youth theatre program! That's OK, though, because a donor is happier giving a $1,000 to a $25,000 program than to a $1,000 program. Your cash needs must be a small portion of your total budget.

It's best, if you are at sea in this area, to hook up with a money person who knows this arcane science of budgeting and have her help you draw up your program budget. Once you get the hang of it, you'll be able to revise it to suit the needs of the moment over the years to come.

Keeping Production/Event Budgets

If you develop a simple program budget, you must remember to develop separate event budgets for each production or performance of your group. Even a quick trip across town to the local elementary school for a ten-minute show with three kids costs your program *something;* figure out what, how that something is paid, and make it into a budget. File it, and be ready to use this data for future funding requests.

Let's say, for example, you are paid $10.00 per hour, are reimbursed $.33 per mile for gas, and use three balloons in the show, at a cost of $.20 each. The agency you work for is 1.5 miles from the school, but you must pick up your actors at the high school, so you end up driving a total of 7 miles to do the ten-minute show, for an agency cost of $2.31. Then, there's the balloons, which together cost $.60. Now, in order to set up the show, which will indeed just be a ten-minute role-play on smoking and peer pressure, you've spent three hours in rehearsal putting the role-play together. Then there's the time needed to get the kids, bring them to the show, do the show, process it with the teacher who invited you, bring the kids back to the high school, or your agency, or their home, and then return to your office. Put that all together, and your agency has paid you about $50 gross salary for the ten-minute show. Since it also must pay taxes, worker's comp, and so on, your agency is probably actually out about $75 salary, plus the cost of the mileage and balloons; round it up to $80. That doesn't count the indirect costs or overhead, training, photocopies, phone, and so forth. To be completely arbitrary, we'll figure those costs at 33 percent of your other costs, or roughly $26.40. That little ten-minute show cost your agency a little over $100. If you do five of those shows a month for ten months of the year, your agency is out over $5,300. But if it ain't on paper, you can't bill for it and you can't ask for a grant to cover it. If it is, you can, and should. So, for you, for your boss, and for your kids, document!

Recording Services Rendered

Another important kind of currency is the actual product you of-fer: the service to your troupe and their audiences. In schools there are lessons plans, attendance records, and grade point averages, which respectively prove the effort (or lack thereof) of the teacher and student on paper. Great teachers can have crappy or nonexist-ent lesson plans and fail to be granted tenure as a result. Brilliant students often flunk courses. Fair or not, it is the paper trail that we are concerned with here, so that your program can prove itself on paper. The author hates to record services on forms. However, it's important. Every rehearsal, group meeting, consultation, and so on with your kids is a service offered, and it should be recorded for the sake of your agency or for prospective funders. You may know that you are doing your kids a world of good, but you have to be able to prove that, for example, you've kept twelve kids off the streets for a total of a thousand hours. Funders don't fund good intentions. Develop a system of recording your services, and up-date it every time you do *anything*! It's a pain, but you can take a few minutes at the computer and do it. The more often you up-date, the easier it is, and it will become habit.

Services to audiences should be recorded separately from ser-vices to your troupe. A five-hundred-person audience is impor-tant to note—numbers count in some funding programs! They can also count in terms of justifying your program to a higher-up. Suppose that you have to justify the program to an agency admin-istrator or school principal? Nothing is respected as much as a re-port brimming with nice numbers. But, again, it is the quality of service that you offer to your troupe that is most important, so you need to devise a way to show that you kept the *same* twelve kids off the streets for a total of 1,000 hours, or 83.3 hours per kid, over a course of twenty weeks. By controlling your data, you can fill out many a grant application in truly impressive fashion. None of this is fun, and it seems to be meaningless paperwork that takes you away from your *real* work, until you miss out on an opportunity because you don't have the proof that you have done good things with your kids.

Funding Your Program

Probably, once you've drawn up a budget, you'll find that you do indeed need to raise some cash. (Again, obviously there are those who will be blessed with a deep-pocket program, but the rest of us have to find some bucks . . .).

Grants and Foundations

Grant and foundation funding *can* be successfully sought. This type of youth theatre program is unique in that it can be funded from several possible areas: the arts sector, the education sector, the public sector, including law enforcement, and the prevention/human services sector.

The New York State Council on the Arts has established an Arts Decentralization Program. The intent of this program is to bring arts away from the established center of artistic activity, New York City, and to develop new and untraditional audiences for the arts. The focus of decentralization funding is on simple, "doable" projects that bring nontraditional or often underserved audience populations into contact with working artists. The author wrote a decentralization grant to partially fund the youth theatre conference that is mentioned earlier in this piece. A warning about funds from the arts sector: the budgets for these programs have been slashed in recent years, and competition for even very small grants is quite high. You must be able to demonstrate key personnel with a proven track record in the arts as well as a program that closely follows grant program guidelines if you expect to receive any funding from these sources. An excerpt of the narrative for a successful arts sector grant application is presented at the end of this chapter.

The author wrote another grant application for Asset Forfeiture Funds, for the long-term program that culminated in the youth theatre conference. This means that we got money from the world of law enforcement to do theatre with kids, and not a single policeman was involved. It's possible. Again, for your edification, an excerpt from a successful proposal is provided at the end of this chapter.

In the case of these two grants, each fed the other in a house-of-cards structure that, amazingly enough, succeeded. It should be noted that the project that developed didn't exactly fit the description in either of the aforementioned grants; for one thing, part of the "standard" Arts Decentralization process is a chipping away of the original request, so two performance evenings became one. However, a mere performance evolved into a day of workshops, with youth trainers, so in a sense the council delivered more than it promised. It is always wise to attempt to structure funding requests in such a way that you can easily meet, if not exceed, goals. By so doing you will in the future show yourself to be worthy of continued funding.

Praise and Honors
Most funders like to be publicly thanked. Get those press releases out, often! By letting the world know that you've received five hundred dollars' worth of stuff from Consolidated Frog, Inc. (which is owned by one of the kids' parents), you will make the giver happy and increase the local community prestige of your program. People give where others have given. Blow your own horn, and honor your funders! One proviso: The long-suffering small retailer who is too generous for her own good may *not* want to be publicly thanked for the donation you weaseled out of her. Check with the boss of the store before you write a release.

Just in case you don't know much about writing a release: Often your local paper will periodically hold workshops for non-profits on this subject. You should know the policy of your agency. You may need to clear any release going out or have it be issued by someone other than yourself who acts as your school's or agency's contact person. It is important that a release be properly formatted, or it simply will end up in the round file.

It is fairly common that nonprofit fund-raisers are followed up by press releases that proudly proclaim the amount raised. Here's a nasty little secret: Usually, these amounts are *gross*, not *net*. The agency dinner may have netted only a fraction of the amount published in the paper. But it looks good, and the givers receive increased self-esteem, and they're more apt to give next time as a result.

Youth-led fund-raising may prove to be an effective way to continue building your group, but it will probably not yield any significant amount of funding. In other words, a bake sale may be a great way to get the group together, but it would be more cost-effective to have the poor parents who have to bake the cookies simply write a check for the amount of the ingredients and let it go at that. As previously mentioned, a haunted house, a novelty that is actually fun, can really make money. But you can unintentionally make enemies in the local nonprofit sector if you horn in on existing fund-raisers. Check the local event scene carefully, then brainstorm ideas for fund-raising events.

Deciding How and When to Charge

It is most reasonable to charge a fee for performances that will cover expenses incurred, but try to resist the temptation to see these requests as opportunities to cover the *entire* cost of your performance. For one thing, the people who are apt to ask your group to perform are likely to be as broke as your agency is, and for another, you must always keep the focus on the process, rather than the product, for the good of your actors. Your actors *need* to do shows—it's a big part of why they are involved.

It also may be, if you use this book and other resources wisely, that you will become locally known as an expert in this field. Then people will ask you to provide training for their agency or school. Don't train for free; it's just plain bad business. It cost you time and money to learn what you know. Charge! Then, send 10 percent of your gross receipts to the author of this book. I will remember you in my prayers.

As for the question of charging your *actors*, now that's another thing. I have always avoided this, so that programs could be accessible to the widest possible range of participants; however, there is something to be said for a small membership fee, as many believe it increases the individual students' buy-in to the group. In America, something we don't pay for *can't* be viewed as anything worthwhile, at least for many. Some successful programs for low-income families charge a token fifty cents or dollar for what are in actuality very expensive programs for this very reason.

As mentioned earlier, everybody knows how to do a bake sale. You might consider asking your group's families to contribute cash to that non-bake sale. It's much easier, as nobody has to bake anything and nobody gains any weight. The families simply donate to the program what they would have spent on Betty Crocker, and everyone calls it a day.

Doing a Site Survey

If you play a hall that is unfamiliar to you, you must take a tip from professional theatre groups and do a site survey of the space in which you are asked to perform. You need to know about the availability of power, lighting, the size of the room, seating, entrances and exits, and so on. Nobody else knows the physical needs of your show or how to present it. So, *go look at the space in person*. If you need a twenty-by-twenty-foot space for your kids' stage, and you ask the nice church lady who's booking you, she will tell you that there is "plenty of room." When you get there, you'll discover that the "stage" in the church basement is only eight feet deep, twelve feet wide, and has a grand piano on it. Church Lady doesn't mean to lie; she just doesn't measure well.

Finding Audiences

Who is your audience? School groups, youth groups, service organizations, church groups . . . once you start, you'll find that you have more potential audiences than you can handle. Youth conferences are always hungry for youth performance groups. Politicians love to have their pictures taken with shining young faces, so don't forget to investigate upcoming events at the state capitol, if you live close enough, or the county seat, or city hall.

Tailoring Your Show to the Audience

The Northway Construction Company's *Life in a Day* became a popular show. We were invited to perform at a Methodist church mother-daughter dinner. The twenty feet we needed turned out to be the space described earlier, complete with the piano. We dealt with it. There was no power for the lights. We dealt with it. Then, halfway through the show, I realized that the vignette about learning there is no Santa Claus was coming up. I looked out at the audience of mothers and their daughters, many as young as six, and felt a cold chill clench my nether regions. There was nothing I could do to stop it. I was in the back of the room, separated by the audience from the actors. I watched in horror as my youth theatre proclaimed the nonexistence of Santa to little children in a church basement. Now, I happen to be a Methodist, and I am reasonably sure that Santa is not part of Methodist theology. But I assure you: hell hath no fury like a mother whose child has been wised up to grim reality by a bunch of teenagers. Be careful what your show says, to whom. It's a jungle out there.

Sample Grantspeak

The following excerpts are taken directly from two grant applications that described the same process slightly differently, so that funding could be obtained from two sources. They're included here so that you can think of ways to massage a grant application, changing your pitch to allow you to do what you want to do.

Example One

Michael Burns, Prevention Education Specialist for the Council, will work over the first four months of the year with the Spaha theatre group to develop a one-hour theatre piece about alcoholism/other drugs.

The piece will be developed using a format loosely based on the Living Newspapers of the WPA Federal Theatre et al. By developing this project, the Council, working in cooperation with Spaha, will instruct a group of young actors in improvisational acting techniques, dynamics of ensemble theatre, dramatic structure/dramaturgy, and the use of theatre as a medium for social commentary.

The piece will be performed in Saratoga Springs, either in the SPAC Little Theatre or in a school auditorium, during a weekend in May. There will be two performances. At each the general public will be able to buy seats, but the main thrust of audience targeting will be at the high school students of the Saratoga

County region. By promoting heavily to school populations, and by encouraging the busing of student groups to the play, the Council will be reaching an audience that has little or no experience with a serious theatre piece that is improvisationally developed by a youthful cast. Although busing will be encouraged through group sales, the Council will not subsidize audience transportation in any way. (ASAC 1993a, 1)

Example Two

POPULATION TO BE SERVED: The Alcohol and Substance Abuse Council of Saratoga County, Inc. will develop a youth theatre project that will operate in the Mechanicville/Stillwater area and Saratoga Springs. In Mechanicville/Stillwater a program will be developed and offered in cooperation with the Mechanicville Area Community Services Center and the Stillwater Community Center; in Saratoga Springs, in cooperation with Spaha, an organization that serves high-risk youth. Teens ages 14–19 will learn about alcohol and other substance abuse addiction, alcoholism/dependency in the family, and the role of substance abuse among peer groups. The goal is to develop "tickler" theatre pieces that will provide raw material for facilitated small and large group discussion. Also, they will receive improvisation and group communication skills.

Projected audiences will include peer groups (e.g., school/youth organizations) and family groups (e.g., parent education programs, etc.).

A. NEED FOR SERVICES: The Council currently offers programs for teens in Mechanicville/Stillwater and Spaha in Saratoga. In each city, approximately twenty youths are involved. Of the youths involved, 100% report that they are from at-risk families. Over 50% report active alcoholism in their nuclear families. Over 80% report previous illicit use of alcohol and other substances. 100% report strong interest in learning more about substance abuse. A recent needs assessment conducted in Stillwater for the Community Center indicated that 80% of teens agree with the statement "There is not enough for teens to do in Stillwater." The same assessment identifies alcohol/substance abuse as a major problem in the area.

B. PRIMARY BENEFIT: The theatre program will have the primary benefit of educating the youthful actors, while providing them with a positive activity as an alternative to the drug lifestyle. They will receive information that may enable them to recognize the need for further assistance (intervention, therapy, etc.) in their own lives. The Council will then serve as a referral source. A secondary benefit will be to the audiences, who will receive accurate information in an intellectually accessible package.

Performances of theatre pieces will be made available to area community, civic, educational, and religious organizations. Prevention Education Specialists from the Council will facilitate discussion after performances. In addition, these educators will supply host organizations with literature and materials pertinent to the material discussed.

Similar programs developed in the past by other agencies have shown that live youth theatre performed by peers is a highly effective way to engage a youth audience. Programs such as the Schenectady Girls Club Youth Expression Theater and CAPTAIN of Shenendehowa's Northway Construction Company have performed for thousands of youths, demonstrating the effectiveness of this approach.

C. DETERMINING DESIRED OUTCOMES: Program participants will complete pre-/post-testing to determine factual knowledge of issues covered. In addition, anonymous "lifestyle questionnaires" will track attitudinal changes toward illicit/high-risk use of substances. Based on the outcomes, curriculum material will be continually adjusted. Audiences will fill out written pre- and post-tests of specific information covered (or, in some cases, show learning though small group discussion). Presentations will be adjusted in the event that audience learning falls below an acceptable level. What is learned from the participants and performance attendees will be evaluated in developing new programs and fine-tuning existing ones.

E. NEEDED FINANCIAL RESOURCES: Current costs of training the youth actors are covered by a Task Force On Integrated Projects grant. In order to mount a functioning youth theatre company, approximately $1500 will be required for the purchase of portable lighting/sound support equipment. An additional $2000 will be required for the purchase of videos, literature, and marketing materials and $2000 for further training (specific to facilitation of teen discussion groups) and travel expenses.

OTHER ORGANIZATIONAL/COMMUNITY RESOURCES: The Council is currently funded by TFIP/other OASAS funds. In addition, The William Reed Foundation exists solely to raise funds for the Council. An application is being made to the New York State Council on the Arts Decentralization Program for funds to cover other associated costs of the Youth Theatre project. It should be noted that Arts Decentralization funds may not be used for equipment acquisition. Since youth theatre efforts are highly visible and make "good P.R.," it is expected that further community support, primarily from the business community, will be forthcoming upon establishment of a successful track record.

ONE-TIME EXPENDITURE: The request for Asset Forfeiture Funds will enable the Council to purchase necessary equipment and other material to provide theatre pieces in a variety of locations. Since this equipment is of a durable nature, and since funds spent on training will have a lasting effect on staff efficacy, there is no reason to assume this request will be repeated. The Council anticipates that future literature and administrative costs will be covered through the above-mentioned enhanced community support.

As stated above, the entire focus of the Youth Theatre project will be prevention education specific to alcohol abuse/chemical dependency issues.

Most TFIP program services are conducted in after-school programs and are currently being held at Mechanicville Community Center, Stillwater Community Center, Ballston Area Teen Center, Saratoga YMCAs, and Franklin Community Center. In all areas most participants are high-risk individuals. In addition, it is expected that due to perceived cues in affect (clothing, hair, speech, etc.) there will be a high identification factor for other teens with similar concerns. Past experience would show that there will be an ongoing, informal recruitment of similar high-risk youths who will be attracted to the program. (ASAC 1993b, 1–4)

6 Multimedia

ultimedia is a school word, a construct, an unnatural thing. Life is, of course, multimedia, as a matter of course, and so is theatre. But it's a useful term to lump together a bunch of things that you can use to make nifty theatre with your troupe. That said, let's take a look.

Placards, Signs, and Banners

We can thank Brecht for these in modern theatre. Simple phrases or words, supporting your topic, introducing scenes, even expressing characters' inner thoughts or emotions, can be carried, waltzed, dragged, or thrown about the stage with great effect. In general, kids love to make them, too. They are really helpful in scene transitions but can also be inside scenes.

Be on the lookout for free/cheap lengths of flimsy cloth. I got many yards of free tricot nylon from a closing lingerie mill a number of years ago, which showed up as scenery, banners, costumes—you name it. In the "real" theatre there is a cloth called sharkstooth scrim, which has the quality of being semitransparent if an object is lit by a light source behind the cloth, but it appears opaque when lit from the front. This is how many a Marley's Ghost has materialized in theatres across the land. Well, many flimsy cloths, including the aforementioned nylon and plain old cheesecloth, will approximate this effect.

Surveyors tape, available at the hardware store in several day-glo colors, can be attached to short lengths of wood for a really cool oriental-circus-act type of effect.

The Bludoobludoobludoo Convention of Flashing Back (and Forth) with Cloth

A tribute to those old movies where the flashback starts with a harp glissando and a series of spinning or defocused images: an actor runs/spins across the stage with a length of chiffon or tricot, or whatever, saying "bludoobludoobludoo!" repeatedly while fluttering the cloth. Audiences love this effect. It's sort of like that Rockettes kick line: takes no skill, but impresses 'em every time!

High-Tech and Low-Tech Video

Video can be amazingly useful in a theatre piece. In just the last few years the technology available has exploded. Digital cameras, which a few years ago would have outshone anything owned by your local news crew, can now be purchased for under a thousand dollars. You or one of your kids may have one of these, and a Mac G4, and the knowledge of how to edit video, make presentations, and so on. Cool. If you don't, it's still a possible tool. Back in the dark ages, I edited video with an editing deck. I have also used VCRs and a camcorder with a bunch of kids and was delighted to find the versatility of the medium, once little details like picture quality and transparent edits were disregarded. So, assuming this latter approach, here are some ideas:

In a piece about alcohol/DWI, kids shot footage of a whiskey bottle being broken by stones thrown at it. This footage was displayed on a screen using the VCR's slow-mo feature, and a camcorder recorded the picture on the screen. This footage, grainy and full of moire effect, was interspersed with a montage of shots (created with a VCR and the camcorder's pause feature—what's known to the pros as "crash editing") including Judy Garland singing "Somewhere over the Rainbow," evening news coverage of a fire, pictures (still and video) of the actors/characters in the piece, and print alcohol ads. This was projected on a screen overhead via a video projector while the actors played a (nonrepresentational) scene about "after the prom." The soundtrack was an old Lou Reed and the Velvet Underground song, "Heroin" (1974). In short, the kids made a consciously crude music video, juxtaposing unrelated images designed to produce discomfort about drinking.

In video, as in their role-play, it's almost inevitable that your kids will include cliche or hackneyed images . . . remember the first time you saw the infinite trail of TV screens when you aimed a camera at a monitor that it was hooked up to? But don't worry. It's their piece, and nobody is going to criticize. The video you produce as part of this product is really just electronic scenery, not something to be shown at Cannes.

You might worry about copyright issues if your kids want to use footage from movies or TV. As a responsible author, I will tell you that in a case such as the previously cited *Wizard of Oz* footage, you should always get permission to use that fifteen seconds of sixty-year-old video, which you will show in a school/human services setting to a handful of high school kids. Right? Riiiiii-ight. Actually, if your purposes are for education, you probably do not need permission. A performance for the general public is another story.

A final thought about video: even clumsy crash editing takes serious time. Play with the medium and experiment before you commit to using video as a major element in your production. Barring an extraordinary kid or kids, you will be the editor/producer of video elements.

Audio

One of the biggest problems you will face is the audibility of your performers. There is no easy answer; these are not trained professionals, and the acoustics at some of the venues you are likely to play would make the three tenors run away in abject panic. Some things can help. If you have access to a PA system, look into renting/purchasing three types of microphones: the wireless lavaliere, the condenser, and the pressure zone microphone (PZM). Radio Shack markets cheap but serviceable versions of all three, or you can go more high-end if you have the money. There are pluses and minuses to each of these.

Wireless Lavs

You can purchase a four-mic setup, where each transmits to a crude mixer that goes "line in" to your PA ("line in" is a setting you'll see on the back of the PA). These can pick up interference from air handling systems and other things, which is a drawback. Your actors may have to trade them back and forth if you don't have enough, which is another. A warning: you need to turn these down when the actor is off, so the unintended whisper or backstage conversation isn't amplified. This can be disastrous!

Condenser Mics

Condenser mics, sometimes called *chorus mics,* are usually hung above the stage about three feet above the performers' heads. They are a good general audio booster. It's probably best to use as many as you can afford, placed as close as possible to the performers.

PZMs

Pressure zone microphones are designed to be placed on the floor in front of your actors. They do a pretty good job of picking up voices, but unfortunately they also do a good job with feet. You can minimize this by taping the PZM to the center of a thirty-six-inch square of plexiglass and propping this up horizontally (against a mic stand, for example) in front of the action. This minimizes the footstep amplification. Be aware that if the PZM picks up any speaker sound, you instantly create a major feedback problem, so speakers must be quite a distance out in the house, away from the stage.

Nonelectrical Audio

Rhythm and musical instruments can greatly add to your piece. You can use five-gallon pails, tin cans, wooden blocks, pan lids—take a cheapo-cheapo, kindergarten approach. When I started this work, it was harder to convince kids to go with this approach, but the success of *Stomp* has made this a lot easier. A particularly effective technique, if your troupe has a gifted musician, is to build a corner for this person into your stage plot and give him or her a frame from which various percussion instruments (pots, pans, wind chimes) are hung, as well as a table that might have a keyboard, a couple of recorders, and a toy xylophone. Then accompanying music can be a prominent part of your piece, as it is in the movies. This technique comes to us by way of the Asian theatre and through much of the "alternative" theatre of the sixties and seventies. Playback Theatre also includes this idea. It works, but it takes real time to blend these sound effects in such a way that focus is preserved.

The Old Warhorse: The Overhead Projector

This is a great tool: with either photocopied or computer-generated transparencies, you can add a whole set of slogans, factoids, supertitles—all in the true spirit of the early WPA Living Newspapers! An overhead projector can also be a great source for a shadow play: in addition to the overhead, pointed toward the audience, all the way upstage, you have a couple of actors standing on stage boxes holding a sheet up. Two actors behind the sheet play the arguing parents in the next room, and the actor playing the main character cringes as she listens, in front of the sheet. *Viola!* A highly dramatic scene, made very simply.

Strobes

Sooner or later, some kid is going to suggest using a strobe. First of all, that sixty watter they got at Spencer Gifts won't do what they hope, 'cause it's really pretty dim. But you may want to use it. Beware, however: strobes can cause seizure in some individuals. If you are going to use a strobe, you *must* warn your audience beforehand. Granted, MGM probably won't send the legbreakers out for a few bootlegged seconds of Judy singing (although you never know), but a seizure caused by your theatre troupe is no joke! Ideally, both a verbal and a written warning should be issued.

Putting It All Together

The following is actually a composite, from the 1990 work of the Northway Construction Company and from that 1993 work by the Spaha Performance Group. The latter piece was developed for a Safe Spring conference, stressing the dangers of DWI before prom season to a countywide gathering of high school students. Taking my own advice, I stole heavily from my work with the NCC when directing the Spaha kids. It's an Elizabethan thing, you see.

ENSEMBLE ON STAGE

NARRATOR INTRODUCES TODD (protagonist)
Todd had a great time at the prom, and the party after the prom. Now he's driving home!

VIDEO MONTAGE: BREAKING BOTTLE, JUDY, FIRE, ALCOHOL ADS

AUDIO: LOU REED, "HEROIN"

ACTION: SPOLIN "PART OF A WHOLE" movement, increasingly sloppy, with surveyors tape banners, around and in front of Todd as he tries to drive. Actors narrate alcohol/DWI facts as Part of a Whole becomes wilder and sloppier. Video images closer and closer together, music crescendo, Todd stiffens and falls into the ensemble's arms, (trust fall) they lay him to floor as actors scream. Blackout, cut music, video.

Actor uses handheld scoop with red lightbulb, back and forth like emergency vehicle light.

Actors use surveyors tape like ventilator, with verbal "whooshing" sounds.

Dialogue: emergency medical technicans, ad lib: sodium bicarb, stat! Clear! Etc. EMTs try CPR, then electrical shock. One actor "beeping" like heart monitor. Red light, ventilator "whooshing" and heart monitor beeps slow, then stops. Silence, brief blackout.

A bright halogen light, aimed at the audience, is turned on.

Dialogue: Todd, step into the light!

Todd is helped up, lights come up, bright light trained away from audience. Todd is disoriented.

Overhead projector: Series of prom snapshots.

Todd: where am I/you're dead/how did I get here, etc.

bludoobludoobludoo effect: earlier that night, at the prom . . .

Actors transform to prom scene.

Overhead Projector: Prom slogan "Living the Dream" followed by prom snapshots.

So, this scenario uses most of the effects outlined here, all in a few minutes. You don't have to lay it on that thick, but for the players and audience in question, the result was highly effective. By the way, as long as you don't crunch the process, you're more than welcome to steal any ideas in this book, including scenarios (Elizabethan!), though it's better if your kids know you're stealing it and it's interspersed with their original stuff . . . Speaking of which, let's look at putting your performance piece together.

7 Structuring a Performance Piece

O nce your troupe has started to develop some basic skills, after, say, ten meetings, and exploration of low-budget multimedia is proceeding, it is time to start seriously considering the structure a performance piece might take.

Perhaps the simplest structure, and certainly an excellent way to break in a new performing troupe, is simply a series of skits, introduced by an MC/facilitator. Simple skits about self-esteem, respect for others with differences, resisting peer pressure, and so on can easily grow out of the work described thus far. Performing such a series of skits for an audience of younger children will have great benefits for your troupe. A sample of such a performance in outline form:

Performance for primary students (30 minutes)

1. Introduction: Set up audience participation, introduce players. (2 minutes)

2. Skit One: Chris' Bad Day
   Chris has a bad day; one disaster builds on another. At end of school day Chris is offered cigarette by older kid.

Facilitator gets audience suggestion ("No Don't Smoke it!"). Argues with audience ("But this is the first person to be nice to Chris all day! Are you sure?").

Audience insists, Chris turns down cigarette, several things that were originally part of the bad day are further revealed not to have turned out so bad after all.

Discussion: If Chris had taken the cigarette, how would (s)he have felt? (8 minutes)

3. Skit Two: The Cool Kids
   Three girls always eat lunch together. One day the Cool Kids take a liking to one of the girls. She deserts her friends at the table, going off with the Cool Kids.

   Facilitator: "How would that feel? What is 'cool'? Should they still be friends? Why? Why not?"

   Action resumes: The Cool Kids prove to be too wild for the girl's comfort: they were going to drink beer at a house with no adults home. She returns to her friends. One responds angrily, with "you" messages, storms off. The other sends "I" messages, they make up.

   Facilitator: "What was the difference between the first girl and the second? Which way would you rather be treated?" (8 minutes)

4. Skit Three: The Blind Kid
   Terry, new to the school, is blind. People act as though (s)he is very hard of hearing, mouthing words and yelling.

   Facilitator: "What's wrong here?" Discussion.

   Terry makes a new "friend," who wants to do everything for Terry, even things (s)he can clearly do unaided.

   Facilitator: "Now what's going on?"

   In class, a kid is silently making fun of Terry's appearance and so on. (S)he picks up on it, and is clearly hurt.

   Facilitator: "Why would that kid want to do that? How would it feel to be Terry?"

   Facilitator conducts an exercise for audience. Everyone must untie their shoes, then tie them again—without using thumbs. (Chaos. Get attention again with whistle, bell, etc.) "Can you do it if you help each other?" (8 minutes)

5. Skit Four: Sticks and Stones
An actor starts with "Sticks and stones may break my bones. . . ."
Another replies, "Oh yeah?" and calls the first a name. As actors enter, they are called, then start calling, names, in a "round robin" of bad feeling. Each time a name is called, one being called name drops to floor as though injured. When all are writhing in pain, the first one apologizes and says something positive. This spreads through group, one at a time they feel better. Finally they join hands, saying the following, with each speaking one word: "Names / can / too / hurt / me. I / am / a / special / person." (4 minutes)

6. Actors, lined up in a row, take curtain call. (2 minutes)

Such performances are relatively easy to develop. By acting as facilitator and by having your troupe perform for a younger and suitably impressed elementary school audience, you support and reinforce your troupe. Many groups go no further than this type of performance and are considered highly successful. But there is much more that can be done and—if you want to provide the highest possible quality experience for your troupe—must be done.

Transitions

We've all been to the school play where the curtain is used, and used, and used. After a stilted little scene, *viewed* by seventy-five parents (armed with forty camcorders), and *heard* by no one, the curtain is closed. Suddenly, in the one-inch gap between the bottom of the curtain and the floor, we see the tantalizing evidence of the real and lively drama of the scene change taking place. Around the auditorium, parents whose faces have previously been frozen in a mask of false approval are truly interested, amused, and involved as they crane their necks to watch the rushing back and forth of feet and the dragging of scenery. There is a loud crash, and fifty people wince as one. A loud "SHHHH!" is followed by a whispered and torrential conference, somehow more audible than all the real scenes in the play, which elicits amusement and wonder from the parents. Then, after a few minutes, the curtain opens, and performers and audience alike sink back into their collective coma. No one seems to be aware that the best and most vital part of the show, filled with the greatest creative tension and most real drama, has been hidden, but for that little one-inch strip. What a shame!

Obviously in the kind of facilitated skits just described for a primary school audience, transitions are talked through by the facilitator and audience as the next skits' chairs and props are set. But in a more advanced piece, for an older audience, the transition/transformation is key.

Curtains

If you are working in a conventional auditorium space with a curtain, you will find the curtain, closed, is a great shield for your actors in training. It shelters the stage from the huge, empty auditorium, creating a small and somehow safe-feeling space, unique among the spaces found in schools, churches, and community centers. For performance, however, starting in the very early workshops, I highly recommend that the "curtain" be Spolin's verbal one: scenes should be begun and ended with the spoken-word curtain rather than with the actual closing of the object. This will help set a paradigm that will facilitate the development of transitions as vital parts of the piece, not as big gaping holes in it.

Transformation is the key. If you and your actors can truly master Transforming the Motion early in training, you will be able to evoke transformation as the shift from scene to scene and place to place. Consider the importance to the modern film and video of the cross-dissolve, where one scene blends into another. We, as an audience, demand that the action not start and then stop again, but that it flow. We are trained to accept the abstract. Consider the bludoobludoo effect, or a thousand other transitions your actors can come up with. Don't use the curtain. The transition, the transformation, is what it is all about.

This is important, too, because you are creating a consciously, proudly, almost defiantly low-budget theatre, in the grand tradition of agitprop. The curtain doesn't belong here. Unless, perhaps, it is a homemade one, a patched, self-conscious, clothesline-pulley-operated affair, which, as a deliberate choice on the part of you and your cast, makes a dramatic statement.

Lights

No matter how crude, lights can certainly aid the transition. I stole the Bread and Puppet technique of using a single handheld aluminum scoop light in a big space as a transition device. It's eery and strangely beautiful. Or you may choose a candle, a strobe, a bunch of flashlights—look around. The possibilities are endless.

Auditory Transitions

We've probably all had the dream/waking experience where the tolling of a lighthouse foghorn becomes the clock radio, or the mysterious stranger repeating our name in a sultry come-hither fashion turns out to be our spouse, who is concerned that we are late for work. This can be a wonderful transition on stage, because people instinctively understand it. They also understand bells. Try securely tying a good strong-toned dinner bell to a six-foot length of cord, then (carefully, so it doesn't fly off like the stone from a sling) striking the bell and twirling it around your head. The Doppler effect will make the bell tone seem to oscillate, which can be quite magical. Combine this with the single scoop light and the dream/waking auditory repetition of a word or a name, and you've created a transition that will seem like pure magic.

"And Now, This!"

Who first wrote those three words for a (probably radio) announcer? Certainly we should have given that anonymous soul some kind of reward: She or he changed civilization. With that ridiculous, meaningless cue, we have been trained to mindlessly accept that we are to be swept away from Castle Frankenstein into the kitchen of Madge the Happy Housewife, who will extol the virtues of Boffo Cleanser. Something in that short phrase makes it seem that we would be fools to go make a sandwich right now— we might miss something important! Note that we seldom hear it used to bring us back to the program: the networks and the advertisers are perfectly happy if we go make our sandwich and miss what happens *after* the commercial.

You, dear reader, are probably a member of the second or third television generation, and your students of the fourth or fifth television generation. We are conditioned to accept commercials, and these little thirty-second masterpieces of propaganda can greatly aid your piece. Maybe consider commercials as *intrinsic parts* of your piece.

Other Visual Ideas

You probably know a bit about Brecht and his Epic Theatre. Ol' Berthold changed the world and kept countless college theatre departments busy with his use of signs, songs, and other oriental-inspired bits of fourth-wall-breaking communication. He did us, in this kind of theatre, a huge favor. Consider and use banners, signs, cheerleading routines, chants, songs, snips of projected video; you are free to use any transition, and once your kids get the idea, the sky will be the limit. It is possible that the piece you develop will become virtually kaleidoscopic, constantly changing. There can be a kind of group euphoria that develops when a piece starts to effortlessly flow from transformation to transformation, each one seeming to perfectly augment the one before. But remember: you do have to maintain the focus of the overall piece; as director this is your responsibility. Make sure things don't get too out of hand.

The Spine

Many Stanislavski-influenced directors will talk about the "spine" of a play—the symbol, phrase, or motif that summarizes and catalyzes their interpretation. A central image or motif can be tremendously useful and can naturally lead to transitions. The spine may be the director's private referent, which helps shape the staging and approach, or it may be a more shared symbol or slogan that director and cast consider together. In an off-off-Broadway production I directed in the late seventies of *A Christmas Carol*, I happened to find a metal ring, about thirty inches in diameter, at the curb one day on my way to rehearsal. I had already been thinking of the circle as a symbol of a solstice, of the heavens, and of God. As a symbol, the circle is universal. I brought the ring to rehearsal. The cast and I worked and played with the ring, and it became a window, a door, a wreath, the sun, the moon, and so on. Most eerily, it became the Ghost of Christmas Yet to Come: at the transition point to that segment, the narrator spun the ring on the stage floor. It spun, faster and faster and louder and louder, until clattering suddenly to a stop. (Try it with a quarter; then imagine it thirty inches in diameter.) Scrooge stared at a point about six feet above the floor where the ring had stopped and spoke to that point as if it were the ghost, invisible to the audience. It was a wonderfully scary and theatrical discovery, which made the production. Everybody loved it except the actor who lost that particular part to an inanimate object!

Can you get a youth theatre troupe to the point where they understand and can construct transformational theatre pieces? *Yes*. If you develop a loving, trusting, and disciplined environment, and work with your troupe on the basics of improvisation as outlined in this book, Spolin's work, and other exercises you may know or learn, it can happen. If it does, you'll be doing prevention work, alright: you'll be showing these kids a very wonderful, nonchemical high better than any drug.

Dramatic Structure in a Post-Aristotelian World

As you will recall, Aristotle defined six necessary elements that make tragedy what it is. These are plot, character, diction, thought, spectacle, and music (Aristotle 1978, 13). Certainly, for an effective dramatic presentation to be developed by a youthful troupe, it is safe to expect that these elements should be present. Spectacle and music may not strike you as being entirely necessary, or may seem unattainable, but we shall examine them as doable parts of your dramatic whole.

Further, Aristotle called for a plot to have a clear beginning and middle and an end that was the logical outcome of the beginning and middle (15). Within Aristotelian structure, emphasis is placed on two main parts to a tragedy: the "involvement" and the "unravelling" (36).

It is no longer truly necessary for a plot to have a clear beginning, middle, and end. You may choose to have a performance piece that is entirely episodic, a somewhat more advanced version of the series-of-skits idea outlined earlier, or you may choose to emulate the Aristotelian ideal. Or, perhaps most interesting is to have a beginning-middle-end structure *interspersed* with thematically related but causally unrelated "bits." As for the involvement and unravelling: in each congruent plot element of your performance piece, these elements will of necessity be present to one degree or another. Aristotle defines *involvement* as the "incidents which precede the beginning of the play, and frequently some of the incidents within the play" (36). In modern parlance, we are talking about the *exposition*. Even in a thirty-second blackout skit, exposition is necessary: the audience must know what the setup is if it is to get the joke. The *unravelling*, then, is the unfolding of complications developed from the circumstances set up in the exposition.

Aristotle calls for tragedy to contain a change in fortune of the protagonist from prosperity to misfortune (24). Certainly this can be an effective device in a theatre piece dealing with the dangers of substance abuse, but the simplistic application of this formula is a tendency that at all costs should be avoided. (Your kids won't avoid it. They love broad, sweeping, melodramatic turns of fortune for their characters. But it *should* be, dammit!) Much modern drama calls for not so much a change in fortune for a character or characters as a change in a relationship between two or more characters.

David Shepherd, the visionary who with Paul Sills started the initial Compass Theatre in Chicago (Compass was the starting point for the group that later was to form Second City), developed a curriculum called the ImprovOlympix, which had some flaws but which contained exercises that can be a tremendous guide in developing a performance piece. Each ImprovOlympix "event" was designed to explore a given topic or theme from a different area of technique—song, story, action, progression of time, and so on. These exercises dovetail with Spolin exercises. In Canada, the ImprovOlympix has further evolved into the Improv Games, and many high schools field interscholastic teams. For reasons unknown, this format is rarely seen in the United States.

A particularly useful event in the ImprovOlympix canon is the Time Dash. I have used this event as the starting point in the development of many a piece.

time dash

Produce: To introduce dramatic structure

Group size: Two

Equipment: Chairs or props, as needed

Source: David Shepherd

In three thirty-second or so scenes, two players show a change in a relationship. Each of the three scenes takes place in the same Where. For example:

WHERE: The Staten Island Ferry

WHO: Lovers

SCENE ONE: Spring. A temperate evening. The relationship is new, flirtatious, exciting.

TIME DASH: THREE MONTHS

SCENE TWO: Summer. Stiflingly hot city night. The couple are experiencing tensions. Argument.

TIME DASH: SIX MONTHS

SCENE THREE: Winter. Cold. The relationship is over. The lovers accidentally bump into each other.

Time Dash fulfills Aristotle's call for a beginning, middle, and end and usually is a quickly grasped and accessible way for young people to begin to plot a piece. The preceding example invoked the inherent symbolism of the changing seasons to help illustrate through the behavior of the actors the changing relationship in a highly effective way.

I have used the Time Dash as the method of working with a young troupe to develop a central story line for a play. It is also possible, given an ensemble of eight or more, to develop three separate story lines involving six or more actors.

For the training period, I suggest strict adherence to the Time Dash requirements that the Where remain the same in all three scenes and that each of the scenes be brief. By keeping to these restrictions, your youthful actors will develop a sense of the strength that economy lends to dramatic structure. As the troupe becomes more skillful, it will of course be appropriate to lengthen the scenes and perhaps change the Where.

It should be noted that the earlier example involved the passing of months, but the length of the Time Dash may be a few seconds or many years. One scene developed by members of the Northway Construction Company had a four-part Time Dash, with Time Dashes of several years, showing the changing relationship of a father and his son at a fishing hole. The last scene featured the son, himself an old man, fishing alone. This tremendously moving Time Dash predated the movie *A River Runs Through It*, which featured a strikingly similar through-line, by several years.

If you find a Time Dash that will serve as a possible through-line, your troupe has various avenues to explore. One is the development of supporting scenes, in other Wheres, which will flesh out and support the central change in relationship. This approach fits comfortably with Aristotelian thought.

Another approach, decidedly non-Aristotelian, is to develop scenes that are thematically supportive but have no direct causal relationship to the Time Dash structure. Consider the popularity of MTV. Many music videos combine some sort of visual story with images that have nothing to do with the story but strike an emotional chord in the viewer. Often both story- and non-story-oriented scenes in the video will have absolutely nothing to do with the lyrics of the song. You are working with a generation that has grown up accepting such post-surrealist montages as perfectly mundane. Conventional theatre from the scripted domain often insists that the audience have each and every action on the stage carefully and logically explained, which, in the case of theatre designed for young people, often leads to a patronizing theatre piece that is a crashing bore for its intended audience.

The Drug Show used the Time Dash structure as central spine. Two girls, friends and roommates, obsess about their problems as they watch TV. A commercial for Nuchems promises to "solve all your problems and get you popularity! money! sex!" They try Nuchems and get very high, forget their problems. They become addicted and reach the moment of needing to ask for help. This simple Time Dash structure was interspersed with scenes showing the cynical ad people counting their money between commercial takes; a pharmacist bargaining the price of the Nuchems up instead of down, taking advantage of the girls' confusion; a "brain commercial," which used Spolin's Part of a Whole to dramatize the effects of alcohol on the brain; and so on. Some of the scenes were causally related to the two main characters; some simply connected by the theme of addiction. Signs announcing scenes or scene elements, like "TV" or "PHARMACY" or "ADDICTION AC-CESSORIES," were on a flipchart on stage. Although some scenes were only related to the story of the two girls in the abstract, the play, as developed, had a lot in common with Aristotelian dramatic structure. The girls were neither perfect nor villains. Through their own actions, yet not entirely through their own fault, they brought misfortune on themselves. They realized their error. Oedipus Rex is roughly congruent.

Shepherd uses the three-sentence structure in his workshops to outline plot. According to this scheme, almost any story can be reduced to three simple sentences. For example, *Romeo and Juliet* would be: "Boy and girl are from warring clans. They fall in love. They die." Once a story is established, plot can be figured out. It may be that your group will start their plot at the end of the story, using flashbacks to demonstrate events leading up to the critical moment. Encourage students to boil their favorite movies, TV shows, and plays down to three sentences and identify the manner of plotting. By so doing, their dramaturgical skills will greatly increase.

An epic, as opposed to tragic (Aristotle 1978, 38) plot may be the way to go. In this case, a sweeping number of characters and events are presented, still within beginning-middle-end structure.

The first thirty-minute beginning-middle-end-structure theatre piece developed by the Northway Construction Company was in response to a request for a performance for a teachers conference. The company was asked for a piece that would cover "a day in the life of a typical high school student," showing pressures and so forth from a "student's-eye view." In brainstorming, the company came up with *A Life in a Day* (not very original, but it seemed to be to these high schoolers).

A Life in a Day followed a group of students through two interlocking time structures: the years kindergarten through twelfth grade, and early morning to after school.

The actors were costumed in basic black outfits to which velcro strips were sewn. At the start of the play a scrap of brightly colored cloth was attached to each piece of velcro. Through the course of the piece, as each hurtful or embarrassing moment occurred, the actors ripped a piece of colored cloth off the injured party. By the end of the play the costumes were uniformly black, and the actors "graduated."

During the course of *A Life,* a kindergarten teacher was played by one actor on another's shoulders (a transformational staging that can be seen to descend directly from "First Lecturette: Authority"). Another teacher was besieged by his own inner voices (two players holding up his desk, a scrap of one-by-eight-inch lumber, and two standing behind him). As the teacher attempted to help a student with the concept of "subtext," the inner voices chanted phrases like "My wife wants a divorce!" "Car payment!," "I Can't Teach!," and so on.

The shuttling back and forth between the progression of the day and the progression through the grades was facilitated by a character with a metronome, who started out energetic and sprightly but ended up exhausted, metronome at slowest setting, shoving the cast toward "graduation" with a muttered "Get the hell out of here."

A Life was highly critical of the processes of public education. However, by including comedy and a scene wherein a teacher, while struggling with his own demons, worked hard to assist a student, the cast was able to reach the audience of teachers with empathy instead of antagonism. The piece debuted at the teachers conference and received a truly thunderous ovation from the educators. This experience showed the author that there is great value in packaging a vinegary message with a bit of honey.

The physical metaphor of colors being ripped off was arrived at quite accidentally when one of the cast members lost a button in rehearsal. The "desk" came about when someone found a piece of board lying around backstage and used it to do "space homework" for the scene. Using found objects in a creative fashion, the actors supplied Aristotle's spectacle, although perhaps not quite in the way he had in mind (there will be more on this type of discovery in Chapter 8, "Equipment"). Further, the piece contained the song "Happy Birthday," so it also had music. *A Life* is a good example of a piece developed by an ensemble that incorporates elements of Aristotelian epic and non-Aristotelian structure.

Plot Development

It is here that you must wear a number of hats. You certainly must be a facilitator. Brainstorming and discussion will yield fruitful ideas. You may also want to be a dramaturg—that is, a recorder of the plot as it unfolds—or you may *not*. At one time I rigorously recorded all developments in rehearsal and summed up the development of the piece for the actors at the start of each new session. It was discovered that this led to a complacent group of actors who possessed less than an optimal investment in the development of the plot. Consider not recording the plot as it develops and rather recapping at the beginning and end of each rehearsal by pulling the myriad details of construction from the assembled ensemble. While perhaps a scary way to go, it can be a very fruitful one. Or you may choose to have a student serve as dramaturg. If you do, be careful just how many eggs you put into a particular basket. Some people tape their sessions, although that method can be very time-consuming: listening to a two-hour rehearsal after participating in one makes for half a day gone.

Facilitating your group's development of a plot that serves the purpose of educating the audience (and of course, primarily your troupe) is the most delightful challenge you will face. How, for example, does the group come up with an illustration for the higher risk children of alcoholics face when they choose to pick up a drink?

In order to answer this question we need to return to your method of giving your troupe the facts they need to make the theatre piece. Consider that most students are, unfortunately, well trained in the factory school "banking concept" of education, characterized by a narrative approach to teaching. The teacher talks, the students listen. Paulo Friere writes:

> The contents, whether values or empirical dimensions of reality, tend in the process of being narrated to become lifeless and petrified. Education is suffering from narration sickness . . . Narration (with the teacher as narrator) leads the students to memorize mechanically the narrated content. Worse yet, it turns them into "containers," into "receptacles" to be "filled" by the teacher. The more completely he fills the receptacles, the better a teacher he is. The more meekly the receptacles permit themselves to be filled, the better students they are. . . . (1987, 238)

If you scatter a fact here and there about alcoholism during the early stages of training, bringing in written material to reinforce your spoken delivery, and if you further encourage students to research and bring in their own facts on the topic, celebrating and reinforcing the choice of an individual student to bring in a newspaper article or what have you, you will begin to break the bank.

(I'm a ham. I've brought my facts in as commercials, preceded by the nonsensical yet universally respected "And now, this." The kids listen, amused, as long as I don't go over thirty seconds . . . fifteen is better.)

Then, when the process of seriously approaching the development of a piece begins, you can ask the students what they know, rather than telling them what they need to know. The development of a vocal tone that indicates true interest and perhaps some puzzlement about the questions you ask in discussing the topic will greatly free up class discussion. Consider the following on authoritarian classroom contexts:

> But over the century empirical evidence suggests that such reflection about different perspectives in discussion rarely occurs in American schools. Even in literature class many teachers still use the recitation—asking closed questions and evaluating the correctness of student answers—as the main structure of classroom talk (Alverman, O'Brien, & Dillon, 1990; Hoetker & Ahlbrand, 1969). This pattern is quite consistent with the tendency to teach and test discrete facts and skills in our educational system. Studies of literary instruction often describe how students are cut off from their own sociocultural response and thinking by teachers insisting on their own "correct," culture-bound translations. . . . (Miller 1992, 2)

The following dialogue is intended to show the way your discussions might lead to plot elements. Bear in mind that by this time your troupe will be well aware of the difference between showing and telling.

Director: So, teen alcoholism. What've we got so far? . . . Well?

Bill: What do you mean?

Director: Teen alcoholism. What have we got? That we can use?

Bill: You mean, like facts and stuff?

Director: Yeah.

Maureen: (*Springing to attention, jokingly reciting*) Ten percent of Americans become alcoholics!

Director: Is that right?

Jim: Isn't it 10 percent who drink become alcoholics?

Director: Is it?

Maureen: Is it or isn't it?

Director: I don't know. It's your show. Who thinks it's 10 percent of those who drink? Who thinks it's 10 percent of Americans? How many Americans drink, anyway?

Bill: Who knows?

Director: What do we know?

Lisa: Alcoholism is a disease.

Director: OK. So?

Lisa: So . . . it isn't anyone's fault. It's like catching a cold. (*General laughter*)

Director: Is it? Like catching a cold? Can you catch it?

Lisa: I don't know.

Bill: No! There's no virus! It's—

Maureen: Wait a minute—isn't it genetic?

Director: Here's some stuff. There was something in here about that. Want to look through?

Maureen: Not really.

Director: Who does?

Maureen: I was just kidding. Give me that.

Director: OK. What if we all go through these pamphlets and see what we can come up with? Here. One for you, and you, one for you. . . . (*The group studies for a few moments.*)

Maureen: It is genetic. They think. At least, it runs in families. Listen to this: "Children of alcoholics face a higher risk than the general population of developing alcoholism." So you get it from your parents!

Lisa: My dad says you get it from your children. (*General laughter*)

Director: So, what do we have that we can show an audience?

Bill: We could do a kid taking sips from his dad's beer.

Director :   How old a kid?

Lisa: Young . . . the younger you are when you start, the higher the risk.

Director: Yeah? Where'd you get that?

Lisa: It's in this pamphlet.

Director: So, how old?

Lisa: Five.

Director: Who's the kid?

Bill: I'll be the kid.

Director: Who's the father?

    Lisa: I'll be the father. (*General laughter*)
Director: Why not? Or would you rather play the mother?
    John: Alcoholics can be either male or female. . . .
Director: OK, you guys, set up a Where, time of day, activity. Show us a five-year-old taking sips from his parent's beer. Lisa will play the parent, either father or mother. You've got two minutes. In the meantime, group, what else do we know about teenage alcoholism? Did anyone track down that 10 percent fact anywhere? . . .

Out of this discussion comes a very short but highly useful scene showing a preoccupied parent working on taxes and a child, bored and lonely, taking sips of beer after requests for attention are denied by the parent.

It is at this point that our discussion should return to psychodrama. In essence, any good drama will present something of the psychodramatic to the participant and audience. It is certainly acceptable for emotions to be liberated as a result of the creative process. But great care must be taken to prevent an uncontrolled reversion into a traumatic childhood experience. Reading the room will help you prevent this type of occurrence. A student who suddenly grows extremely quiet or one who suddenly becomes highly emotional in a scene should be gently asked if everything is OK. If everything is *not* OK, the activity should be stopped for the moment, and the student briefly spoken with. If a high degree of trust exists in the group (which it should), and if students feel they have permission to opt out of any exercise (which they should), the student may stop something that starts to hit too close to home. At no time should a student be urged to go on in a scene that is becoming uncomfortable! However, taking the student aside later and discussing the issue privately is the only responsible course of action. If the student discloses something about home life that indicates a problem, you are in a unique position to make a referral to appropriate counseling/ treatment. I have referred numerous acting students as a result of this kind of gentle probing.

In my home state, New York, anyone who works with youth in a school or an agency is de facto a mandated reporter, legally required to notify Child Protective Services if there is a concern about possible abuse. Usually, the reporter is not the actual contact with Child Protective Services; that's up to an agency administrator or building principal. But the report must be made by the youth worker to that supervisor, by law. It is probable that you are a mandated reporter, or the equivalent, in your locality. Therefore, you are bound by law to report suspected child abuse to the proper authorities. It is quite important that your young actors understand that you can and will keep any confidence *except one that indicates that the student or another is in danger.* This includes students' reports of physical, sexual, or emotional abuse at home as well as reports of suicidal feelings. Making clear from the start that this is the case will help you immeasurably when the disclosure of abuse comes forward from one of your students. Being trapped into a blanket promise to keep a secret is an absolute no-no.

Recycling: Take an Elizabethan Approach

Remember your homework at the beginning of this book, to watch *Shakespeare in Love?* Cool movie, which captures much of the timeless flavor of a troupe. However, the movie strayed from truth often, including its depiction of Shakespeare stumbling into the plot for *Romeo and Juliet.* That story was around for a long time, and the Bard simply stole it, names and all. No big deal in Elizabethan England, and actually no big deal today.

There are no new stories. It's really that simple. If you consider the three-sentence story outline, all of our plays and movies boil down to a paltry few stories . . . a few hundred. It's what we *do* with them that's new. So if you're uncomfortable 'cause your crew is re-creating a Romeo and Juliet scenario, don't be! They won't end up plagiarizing the Bard, just borrowing from him in a fashion that he would have approved of.

This does not mean that I am advocating plagiarism—I'm not. Whenever possible, quotes and paraphrases should indeed be cited. What I am saying is that your group's treatment of a given story line will perforce differ sufficiently from the model to not be considered theft.

As an experiment, some years ago, I based a piece on a written scenario I had been shown by David Shepherd. The piece was called *Georgina's First Date* and was originally written by Elaine

May and acted by the original Compass Theatre in Chicago. We intended to credit May in the program: "Developed improvisationally, from a scenario originally written by Elaine May for the Compass Theatre." I laid out for my actors the scenario, we started rehearsing, and . . . it became something else entirely. Transformation. The piece was still about high school angst, but had little if anything in common with the scenario I had presented to the group. I altered the program note to read: "Developed improvisationally, *loosely based* on a scenario. . . ." So if you (or your troupe) come up with a story line that is (to you) uncomfortably similar to *Annie*, for example, what of it? Do you really think *Annie* was original? Would Charlie Chaplin think so if he were alive to see it? Would Will Shakespeare? Especially given the explosion of unattributed folklore being forwarded furiously about the world by email, we are living in a culture in some ways similar to Elizabethan England. Go with the flow, cite when you can, and don't worry . . . it all works out somehow. . . .

As director/dramaturg/facilitator/producer, you will do a lot of actual or virtual writing of the piece that is developed. There is nothing wrong with this. I urge you, however, to keep an open mind, and be willing and ready to drop or modify your ideas if the kids come up with something that would work as well (or even almost as well) as your idea. This is their piece. I personally like to slide a lot of ideas in that the kids pick up and make their own. They will quickly forget that the originator of the bludooobludoo effect, for example, was moi, and own it as their own. As it should be. You should and probably do have an ego strong enough to enjoy the lack of awareness of how many of your ideas are in the final product. Bear in mind, before you get too smug about that secret knowledge, that you probably stole those ideas from somebody else. It's an Elizabethan thing. . . .

Playback Theatre is a form developed by Jonathan Fox that incorporates personal story into an improvisation instantly, in ritual fashion. The resulting theatre is "essential theatre"; that is, it seeks to reflect the essence, not the details, of the story related. Playback uses a conductor, rather than a director. The conductor acts as a sort of emcee/facilitator, helping the teller, who may be an actor or an audience member, cast the instant enactment of the story.

In Playback, the only props are pieces of cloth, which may be used as symbols for clothing, feelings, signs, buildings, environments, and so on. In addition to the teller and the conductor, there are five actors and a musician.

In a Playback experience, the teller relates a personal story. The conductor assists the teller in identifying and casting the roles in the story. A role may be the feeling of confusion, another may be the street, yet another may be a person. The actors enact the story immediately, while the musician provides accompaniment.

Please do not try to use Playback based solely on this description. It is an elegantly simple form, but the previous brief description does not do it anything approaching justice. If you live in the Northeast, you will want to inquire about classes at the School of Playback Theatre. You can learn more about this form on the web at <www.playbacknet.org>.

Playback should be introduced to your troupe after they have developed a sense of the transformational nature of improvisation and have shown some facility at true improvisation. I have introduced Playback successfully to a group that met twice a week after the eighth training session. Stressing that this is *not* Spolin work, that it is another way into the improvisational experience, and encouraging the actors to develop a sense of playfulness and spontaneity within the personal and symbolic world of the Playback modality proved to help the group have an energizing and catalytic experience.

Time for a caution: Playback exists somewhere between Spolin et al. and the work of the psychodramatists. Since personal story is the basis for the Playback experience, you need to be grounded in a safe and trusting environment before you engage in this part of a group's training. You also should be guided through the Playback experience by an experienced trainer before you attempt to train others. If it is possible to be trained at Fox's school, by all means do so! If it is not, at least be in touch by mail with the school and read up on the subject thoroughly before you proceed.

Much of what has been discussed in this chapter is the result of the Living Newspaper, a theatrical form that can be traced directly back to the Federal Theatre of the Great Depression in America and indirectly to the early Soviet Agitprop Theater of the Russian Revolution. Living Newspapers combined sketch story lines with "The Voice of The living Newspaper," a verbal headline, and large overhead projections. These pieces of educational and political theatre were avant-garde in the thirties, and, as has been previously mentioned, scared the professional actors involved in them. But *your* actors have grown up in a world where the Living Newspaper has left its mark everywhere. A Living Newspaper on a given topic might be a great choice for your first major production. If you haven't heard of or read much about the Living Newspapers, do some research. It's a richly rewarding topic.

One of the Living Newspaper plays, *Spirochete*, dealt with the then-incurable disease syphilis. During the nineties, Caroline Anderson, a professor of theatre at Skidmore College, cowrote with Wilma Hall *Faces: A Living Newspaper on AIDS. Faces* has been performed in several venues, by several companies. Each time it has been a different play, but each time it has been full of important information about HIV.

8   Equipment

There's a wonderful scene in *A Midsummer's Night Dream* wherein the "rude mechanicals," Bottom and the other eager amateurs, try to solve the problem of showing moonlight through the window. They settle on the device of an actor clad in a crescent moon hat, holding a lantern and explaining that he is the moon. One of the real charms of what Peter Brook calls "rough theatre" (1968, 65) is the use of crude, sometimes even ridiculous, technical effects. In my opinion, you and your troupe should embrace this as a method, but *consciously*. In other words, try to help your actors understand that you are making a deliberate point of creating technical theatre with the bones showing, so to speak. This choice frees you immensely. The following items have helped many theatres create magic for next to nothing.

Rehearsal Boxes

College theatre departments always have these on hand, as do many professional theatres. Some people like to build these out of half-inch ply, with all six sides closed. This yields a stable but bulky and difficult-to-move item. They are usually sixteen or eighteen inches square. Better than the totally closed box are two types of open boxes, one with five sides and the other with only one side plywood, the other five sides open. Type one is great for carrying props; type two, being completely open, lends itself to innovative staging (for example, four of them stacked, with the closed side away from the audience, become a cage for an actor).

To build a type two box, using the best available 1 × 2, build four rectangles, each 15.25 inches by 15.5 inches. Join these together, using screws and glue or a biscuit joiner, to make a cube. Top with half-inch ply. You should end up with a 16-inch square cube (see Figure 8–1).

Stage Boxes

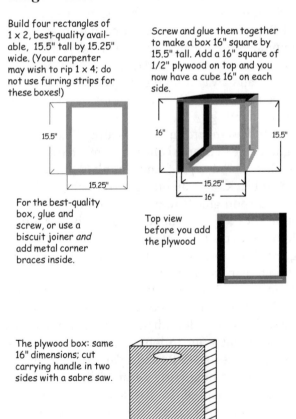

Build four rectangles of 1 x 2, best-quality available, 15.5" tall by 15.25" wide. (Your carpenter may wish to rip 1 x 4; do not use furring strips for these boxes!)

15.5"

15.25"

For the best-quality box, glue and screw, or use a biscuit joiner *and* add metal corner braces inside.

Screw and glue them together to make a box 16" square by 15.5" tall. Add a 16" square of 1/2" plywood on top and you now have a cube 16" on each side.

16"

15.5"

15.25"

16"

Top view before you add the plywood

The plywood box: same 16" dimensions; cut carrying handle in two sides with a sabre saw.

Figure 8–1

Type two cubes are very light and can also be used for nifty low-tech lighting solutions—draped with scrimlike fabric, such as cheesecloth or tricot, with backlighting, for example.

You can also drill a hole or attach a flange on the inside of the the hard side of either type to make a standard (support) for a length of dowel, a flag or banner, and so on. Experiment!

Lighting

If you are thinking about lighting for visibility, don't worry about it. Turn on the lights in the room. Theatre got along just fine for thousands of years with just daylight. However, if you're searching for theatrical effects, here are some ideas.

Peter Schumann, the genius puppeteer and director of the Bread and Puppet Theatre, can do amazing things with a hand-held aluminum clip-on scoop lamp, the kind you buy at the hardware store for five bucks. In a darkened room, moving this up, down, toward, and away from the subject can be incredibly theatrical. The point? You may not have a lot of money, but you *can* have dramatic lighting.

A homemade standard in poor theatre of various kinds is the tin-can light, made of a large coffee or number 10 can, a two-piece ceramic socket, a cord, a plug, and a hunk of plumber's strap iron. Spray painted black, with an outdoor spotlight (PAR) lamp, these approximate a spotlight. However: you should check the various Web auction sites . . . you might be able to buy real rock 'n' roll–style PAR instruments really cheap!

I suggest PARs, preferably smaller ones, like PAR 38s, 'cause they are tough, hard to damage, and your student actors will find them easy to focus. The downside is that they can't be shuttered or goboed, but that stuff gets too complicated anyway!

The same holds true for a light board: cheap used equipment abounds. You might want to look for a two-scene preset, eight-dimmer setup with some PARs and a couple of stands. You should be able to find something fairly cheap. Defunct rock bands often have lighting equipment of this nature to sell cheap.

If you must go *super* cheap, the old reliable household dimmer, ganged in work boxes with receptacles, can make a simple light board. You'll need to trim the cover plates a bit with a band saw or grinder so they'll fit together, and make sure you don't gang more than three, because of possible heat buildup. Also, *never* overload dimmer capacity: if you do, the dimmer will become merely an on/off switch. It is safest to load only to 75 percent of dimmer capacity—in other words, no more than 450 watts on a 600-watt dimmer.

You'll notice the descriptions here are even sketchier than they are for the carpentry stuff. With electricals, if you can't do it from these suggestions, don't! Find a qualified electrician or handyman, so you don't burn the joint down or produce a shocking theatre piece!

You may need to find or make stands for lights, if your troupe is on the road. Again, I strongly recommend used equipment off the Web—there's a lot out there. If you must make do with other ideas, check into the following:

Will the local school's phys ed department let you borrow volleyball net standards? These have a weighted base that is wheeled for ease of use, and often the uprights are in two sections, which facilitates shipping in a van or a pickup. If so, you can mount your lights to a length of conduit attached via a T connector to an eight-inch nipple that will slide into the top of the pipes. (If this paragraph mystifies you, wander around the plumbing/electrical section of a good hardware store.)

Don't forget the obvious, around-the-house items you can use for dramatic effect: Christmas lights, candles (careful!), flashlights, and so on. That old super-eight movie light with a halogen lamp up in the attic can pack a whallop, but just make sure you apply safety/commonsense rules.

Recently the Christmas lighting industry has introduced little outdoor spotlights designed to project an image on the side of the house. These can be very useful. Shop the discount stores in January!

Stage Flats

Conventional interior box sets are usually primarily made of flats and platforms. I recommend a minimalist style, as you know, but you may find limited use of flats to be handy. A flat can be a projection surface, or it can provide an entrance: a couple of flats on either side of your stage area can make a proscenium, if you are working in a nontraditional performance space.

Usually, flats are built in stock four-foot widths, and stock eight-, ten-, twelve-, or sixteen-foot lengths. For a traveling youth troupe I suggest building three-foot-by-six-foot flats, so you can get them in and out of a minivan easily. There are two basic types of flats: (1) the muslin flat, where the 1 × 3 boards are flat side out, braced with quarter-inch plywood on the back, and covered with stretched, painted muslin and (2) the TV flat, which is like a shadow box, with the 1 × 3 sides faced by quarter-inch plywood, which is then painted.

Whichever kind you build, use the best wood you can afford. It's better to rip 1 × 4 into 1 × 3 than to use furring strips, which tend to warp and split. Use sheetrock screws to build your flats.

On its own, a plywood (TV) flat is a remarkably stable, paintable, and reusable item. To make it fancy, you can build flats that contain windows and so on.

You may want to build a couple of jacks to hold the flats up. These usually are attached with small loose-pin hinges, and the bottom is weighted down with a stage weight or a sandbag. If you have no stage equipped with these, you might buy swimming pool filter sand, which comes in a tough plastic bag. These are quite heavy, though—it's better to try to borrow a couple of metal stage weights from a local theatre.

Periaktoi

The periaktos is an incredibly useful device invented by the ancient Greeks. (The plural, periaktoi, has become the default name for these babies, even when only one is used, but some literate types will cringe if you refer to one periaktoi.)

A periaktos is basically a revolving prism. You can make one very simply by using loose-pin hinges to attach three standard (muslin) stage flats together. On the bottom, attach three casters. You can cover the piece with three solid sides of muslin, cardboard, or quarter-inch ply, or you can leave one or more sides open. You can put a shelf in the unit to hold props, or have a completely open third side for an actor to use as a door. (See Figure 8–2.)

Periaktos, deluxe version:

Buy three of the best-quality casters you can afford, with good rubber wheels.

Cut six pieces 1 x 6, 72" long. Using a table saw, bevel one edge of each at a 30-degree angle. These are screwed together with 1.5" sheetrock screws, to form the three corner caps.

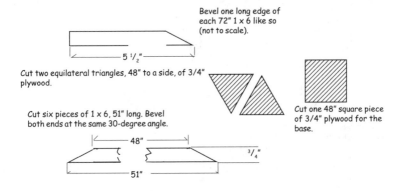

Bevel one long edge of each 72" 1 x 6 like so (not to scale).

Cut two equilateral triangles, 48" to a side, of 3/4" plywood.

Cut six pieces of 1 x 6, 51" long. Bevel both ends at the same 30-degree angle.

Cut one 48" square piece of 3/4" plywood for the base.

Make three 36" x 72" muslin-style flats, like this, using 1 x 3 and 1/4" ply corner braces and keystones, like this. Use 1" screws to attach braces.

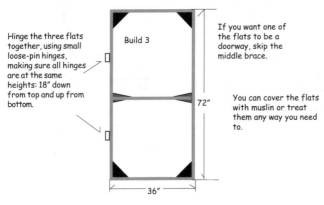

Hinge the three flats together, using small loose-pin hinges, making sure all hinges are at the same heights: 18" down from top and up from bottom.

Build 3

If you want one of the flats to be a doorway, skip the middle brace.

You can cover the flats with muslin or treat them any way you need to.

72"

36"

Figure 8–2

Continued on next page

By dressing each side differently, you can suggest a number of different visuals/Wheres simply by rotating the periaktos sixty degrees. Three periaktoi, a few stage boxes, and a stool or two can make a striking and versatile all-purpose set. Part of the beauty of

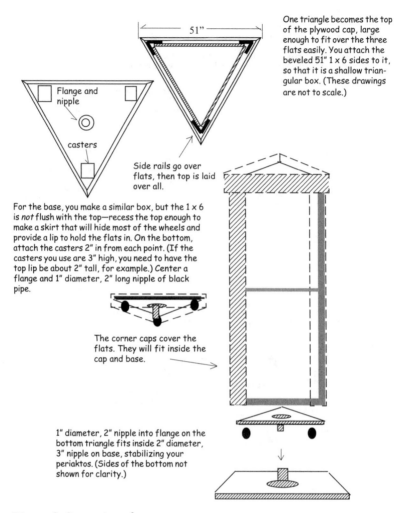

One triangle becomes the top of the plywood cap, large enough to fit over the three flats easily. You attach the beveled 51" 1 x 6 sides to it, so that it is a shallow triangular box. (These drawings are not to scale.)

51"

Flange and nipple

casters

Side rails go over flats, then top is laid over all.

For the base, you make a similar box, but the 1 x 6 is *not* flush with the top—recess the top enough to make a skirt that will hide most of the wheels and provide a lip to hold the flats in. On the bottom, attach the casters 2" in from each point. (If the casters you use are 3" high, you need to have the top lip be about 2" tall, for example.) Center a flange and 1" diameter, 2" long nipple of black pipe.

The corner caps cover the flats. They will fit inside the cap and base.

1" diameter, 2" nipple into flange on the bottom triangle fits inside 2" diameter, 3" nipple on base, stabilizing your periaktos. (Sides of the bottom not shown for clarity.)

Figure 8–2 continued

this little piece is that you don't have to worry about stage braces or screws in the floor—remember those custodians!

Found/Transformational Props

You are living in the land of wonder, where more manufactured stuff is thrown away every minute than once was made in a year. If you can snag some, even temporarily, for your theatre, you'll be doing the planet and your kids a great favor. Shredded paper, Styrofoam, packing materials, the list goes on and on. Robots, astronauts, and mythic warriors can all be costumed out of the dumpster.

Always be on the lookout for any of these, and more, if you can find them free or cheap:

large lengths of cloth

mechanic's dollies (the kind you scoot under the car with)

noisemakers/rhythm instruments

cast-off, but functioning, video equipment

art supplies, including odd lots of interior latex paint

interesting old clothing pieces, including hats and halloween costumes

The Prop List

Much of the work described in this book calls for the actors to develop their skill at space work, which is essentially a form of mime. However, particularly with transformational performance pieces, a collection of hand props can be valuable. Consider also the exercise Props: encourage your students to use props transformationally.

A partial list of useful props to keep on hand:

telephone

pots, pans, kitchen stuff

plates, bowls, utensils, and so on

an old TV, cabinet type, with guts removed (this way the audience can look through it, while the actors in a scene "watch" TV—also good as a cabinet, etc.)

lightweight and easy-to-move table

pillows

books/magazines

hand tools of various types

I hope you become a planeteer prop builder, and recycle lots of stuff into your performances. However, be aware of the real danger that your rehearsal and performance space might become a junk shop; if a prop is not used, after a period of time, get it back to the dump or the Salvation Army. Space is important.

[9] In the Residential Facility

I currently work part time as a drama teacher in a residential facility for girls in upstate New York called the Charlton School. Within the Charlton School is the Ketchum-Grande Memorial School, the educational part of the overall facility.

Charlton serves girls in the high school age group (fourteen through eighteen) who are mandated by the court to the facility. It isn't a reform school. There are no bars or locked doors. To the casual observer, Charlton would appear to be a small private girls school, and that's what it is. But the girls are, as a rule, slightly different from other groups I've worked with, and I'm continually learning ways I need to modify my approach to serve them better.

I also spent an intense, but beautiful, several weeks directing inmate-written plays at Greene Correctional Facility in New York State. The young men at Greene had something in common with the girls at Charlton. If you work with a special population, you may have found much of what is described in the previous chapters to seem unattainable. That's not necessarily so, but there probably is a need to adjust the approach somewhat. Let's look at some of the necessary adjustments.

Before we throw phrases from the *DSM IV* (for the uninitiated: the *Diagnostic and Statistical Manual*, fourth edition, the book that doctors, social workers, and insurance companies use to label symptoms and people), let's try to get a working model for the problems inherent in working in a residential setting.

Did you read *Alice in Wonderland?* Remember the croquet game? The flamingos, which served as mallets, were biting and arguing, and the hedgehog balls just got up and walked away. If you undertake work in an institution, read *Alice* again. Then go down the rabbit hole and prepare to improvise.

Behavioral Rules and Boundaries

I tend to empower youth groups I work with, and actively enjoy being told to go away when a group is "hot" and working on something. However, in the institution, you must first firmly and clearly establish your authority and work within the behavioral guidelines of the place, handing out mandated consequences for behaviors that are not allowed, even if, as an artist, you find the restrictions to seem Machiavellian. It's a matter of personal safety for the students. If you suddenly thrust them into a situation that's clearly outside the rules, so to speak, they will lash out, act out, and generally wreak havoc. Not because they're malicious, just 'cause they need to know where the boundaries are. So be a bit of a control freak, if you aren't usually.

Once a high degree of mutual trust is established, you can bend the rules a bit. But if this happens, it should be acknowledged, so it's understood you are making a choice, not getting sloppy or weak.

A problem: You're going to try to impose a dramatic structure on a group of people, and in fact a culture, for whom a great number of dramas are already being carried out. Be on the lookout for the following attitudes and disorders.

"You can't teach me this; I have never seen this before!"
Kids in placement tend to be very frightened of change and of the new. With good reason. They've been ambushed and bushwhacked by life, and in many cases have developed a coping persona that did help, some, in warding off danger, but probably also got them sent to court. They have to be safe, but would never admit to that need to a stranger. If possible, try to relate the new

thing to something familiar, but stay firm. Don't back down . . . otherwise you'll never introduce anything new.

"I can't do this today. Everything sucks!"

Tell me you can't identify. I teach two days a week at Charlton; one of those days is Monday, when lots of hungover girls have come back from weekend passes. I get this one a lot. Cheerfully identifying, while proceeding, is the way that seems to work most often.

Now, I hate to use labels like ADHD. But let's, 'cause it's easiest that way.

Attention-Deficit Hyperactivity Disorder (ADHD)

If you work in an institution, you are probably aware of the different disabilities that may contribute to your students' challenges. Probably, attention-deficit hyperactivity disorder (ADHD) is rampant; this means you must keep things moving. There are a number of strategies for ADHD kids that can really help. I routinely meet one-on-one with an ADHD kid and set up a contract wherein I will get physically close, if he is zoning out, to provide a visual prompt. It often works. I'm sure you have your own strategies.

Oppositional Defiant Disorder (ODD)

In institutional work, and often in the public school as well, ODD behavior rears its ugly head *all* the time. Handing the power back to the student, I have found, can shortcut a power struggle and break the defiance quickly. Remember that an oppositional/defiant response is a knee-jerk reaction, and *don't buy in.* Many adults meet this type of reaction with a *mirror,* and then the next ten minutes are given over to a power struggle. You do not have time for this! Rather, consider extinction, followed by reflection as a tool. For example:

> Teacher: OK, let's get these chairs out of the way and make a circle.
> Oppositional Opie: I don't wanna make a dumb circle!
> Teacher: That's it, Candace, Great, Jimmy! (*Extinction: You simply don't hear Opie.*)
> Opie: I ain't gonna make a dumb circle!
> Teacher: (*Here, you must come across as surprised, loving, concerned*) What's that, Opie?

> Opie: Don' wanna make a dumb circle!
> Teacher : You don't want to make a circle!
> Opie: You're always having us move around, just when we get set!
> Teacher: I'm always moving you guys around.
> Opie: I'm tired!
> Teacher: You're *tired!*
> Opie: What we gotta make a dumb circle for anyway?
> Teacher: You don't understand why we *need* to make a circle. Well, the next exercise—
> Opie: Don' wanna!
> Teacher: OK. I understand. You don't have to. But we need you to move to the edge of the room, then. I'm really sorry, 'cause I know you're tired, but we need the space.
> Candace: *(Impatiently)* Jesus!
> Teacher: Let's keep the language appropriate, Candace!
> Candace: He's always pulling this!
> Teacher: Opie is tired today. OK, everybody—excuse me, Opie, thank you so much—let's get started with . . .
> Opie: I didn't say I wouldn't do it! I'm just tired!
> Teacher: *(Pleased, but it ain't no big deal . . . don't gloat!)* Oh, you're joining us? Great! OK, here we go. . . .

In this dialogue, Opie was set and ready for a power struggle, which the teacher refused to buy in to. By loving him to death, so to speak, and reflecting on (but not necessarily agreeing with) everything he said, the teacher pulled all the wind from his oppositional sails. Even more important, the teacher let another student get impatient with Opie's nonsense, thus lessening (rather than strengthening) his feeling of power and his perception of group esteem. The difficulty is that the teacher must appear truly concerned with Opie, while keeping the dialogue moving. Any hint of sarcasm in the teacher's tone will let Opie win. One might wonder why Opie is there at all; the simple answer may be that he has nowhere else to be. Give him a space where he encounters an adult who is not authoritarian. He will come around.

Post-Traumatic Stress Disorder (PTSD)

Be on the lookout for the exaggerated startle, which may be followed by rage. Sometimes the rage is preceded by a short period of intense quiet, which may look like sulking. If you get a sense that a kid with PTSD has just been triggered but hasn't gone off yet, see if you can run interference and encourage a time-out. Usually in institutions, kids with PTSD know they need to time-out. If you are a theatre person in this new world, you may recognize this disorder, as you've seen it in theatres and know that sometimes people just need to chill. It's the same in institutions. You shouldn't beat yourself up if someone's PTSD is triggered: it can be over something very seemingly innocent. In general, avoid situations that can produce claustrophobic reactions with all your students, and it's probably a good idea to extinguish skits that conjure up student renditions of the drunken-parent-with-a-belt before they start, unless you are working directly with the institution's therapists, who are in the room with you at the time. There's plenty to dramatize that can expand your students without dredging up past hurt.

Keep It Simple

In general, you need to be more concrete and less abstract in an institutional setting. Whereas a group of kids in the outside world may readily accept, say, the spinning hoop in *A Christmas Carol* representing the Ghost of Christmas Yet to Come, these kids want to *see* the damn *ghost,* period.

Keep It Short and Doable
In a facility, life changes fast. It's probably best to avoid long projects with delayed payoff. Immediate gratification is the key. Video is a great tool: you can watch yourself immediately, which is always a fascination for adolescents. As teacher, you may need to accept that the brilliant scene that occurred in class Monday will never be repeated.

Keep It Fun
In institutional work, thou shalt not bore. I spent an entire semester trying to get my students to learn some basic terms, like

proscenium. They were smart enough to learn, but they didn't *want* to. I was *boring.* Another semester, they knew the word, 'cause I used it during fun activities and never made a point of teaching it. (One of those students, however, always called it "the *prodendum*," which challenged my ability to keep a poker face.)

Build the Skills

This *ain't* simple: Praise, praise, praise, reinforce, and praise some more when a new skill is acquired. They'll soak it up. It may be hard to realize and remember what a risk it is for some kids to engage in any of this whack stuff you frontin'.

Incorporate Dance

Dance is universal. At least with girls, the most sustained effort I've scene is on dance routines. I know next to nothing about dance, but that's OK, 'cause the girls can choreograph themselves. In this case, if you don't know dance, you become a monitor, servant, and cheerleader to the group that is putting a dance together. In the case of dance, I've seen girls get so intensely involved that they verge on violence because of their very real and familiar creative frustration. You are the safety valve; you have to provide the control necessary to avoid this.

Use Trust Exercises—When Appropriate

In the prison, because of the rules, we just couldn't go there. (Inmates were not allowed to touch, which struck me as *both* wise protection of personal safety *and* a highly twisted form of cruel and unusual punishment.) In the girls school, we can, and do. Hypervigilance on your part: impulsive "jokes" can harm. But in general, I've found that the kids in institutional settings love trust exercises and definitely need them. Blind Circle (Chapter 10), Willow in the Wind (Chapter 2), and Clay Molding (Chapter 10) are all usually big hits. You, of course, will be vigilant to keep appropriate boundaries in place as trust work is accomplished.

The Institution as Entity

Public schools are, of course, institutions, and they have their own weird rituals and rules. Residential facilities are usually even more rule-laden and restrictive. Sometimes it may seem that you are spending inordinate amounts of time using keys, acquiring permission, and so forth. Breathe. Pick up your flamingo, grab a hedgehog, and have a go: croquet is a fun game, once you get the hang of it.

Producing in Wonderland

A show is a show is a show, and a show is magic. If you work in an institution, you may have the opportunity to put on a show. Rather than trying for a theatre piece, unified, as discussed in the bulk of this book, consider a talent show. If there is a music teacher, can she develop a singing group or one song? Then maybe a dance routine or two, and if you are very lucky, you can throw a comedy sketch or two together. Perhaps, if you've been using video, you can show a clip or two. Is there a kid that does a really funny imitation of a chicken? Get that kid to do the chicken thing. If you decide to go this route, and have the backing of administration, you will need to develop the little pieces separately, then have at least three big rehearsals, where you have all the acts together on stage, plus someone on lights, and so forth. These rehearsals will test your ability to stay serene. Students will quit; hedgehogs will be strolling everywhere. Resist the urge to become the Red Queen and shout "Off with their heads!" But you may have to yell *a bit*, to be heard. Remember, they desperately want to look good, and they want you to provide the control necessary to allow them to look good.

Over the years I've worked in conventional theatres with a number of stage managers. A stage manager, not a luxury you are likely to have, is like a director's second brain, organizer, taskmaster, and overall supporter of the show. One of the best stage managers I know, Stacie Mayette, who is now general manager of Home Made Theater in Saratoga, has been known to lean over and quietly ask, "Is it time for the tantrum?" Stacie knows the importance of the moment Peter Brook described earlier and is comfortable with a director yelling at the cast—within reason, and for a purpose. In an institution, you can indeed do the same thing, but be aware of the people you are working with and their triggers.

If you are in an institutional setting working with a large group on a rehearsal, demand, if necessary, several other staff members to be present. For some reason, an institution where a five-to-one resident-to-staff ratio is considered dicey will suddenly drop all restrictions and throw a theatre person into a room full of kids to create a show. I've seen this at more than one institution, although my current employer is excellent in this regard.

1O Exercises

A s has been stated before, there are many important exercises in Spolin's *Improvisation for the Theatre* (1999). Some of these are hers; others come from the improv and training work that has flowed around the country since her day, and may incorporate her work or be similar. Whenever possible, I've cited a source. I've also named myself as the source in those instances where I believe I've invented (or changed beyond reasonable recognition) an exercise. I ask all who believe they invented a given exercise first, whom I have failed to credit, to forgive me; I have found it common that we improvisors often duplicate each other's work unknowingly. The descriptions are sometimes written as though a workshop leader is speaking, for the purpose of helping you visualize their use, but please don't read them to the group. Know these well enough that you can use your own words, which will be more alive.

This chapter is arranged in related groups, starting with warm-up exercises, then moving to advanced exercises.

Warm-Up Exercises

general warm-up

Purpose: To encourage general relaxation, centering

Group size: Any

Equipment: None

Source: Assembled by Michael Burns, derived from numerous commonly used warm-ups

First, have everybody get in a circle. Have everyone breathe for a minute. Nothing else, just breathe. The "actors" in the group will want to demonstrate their knowledge of the importance of stretching muscles, and so on; try to gently encourage them to drop all of that for a moment, and just *breathe.*

Now, ask the students to stretch—reach way up for something above their heads, just out of reach of their hands, stand on tiptoes and see that thing they want, just out of reach. After a moment, ask everyone to drop their hands and relax.

Have them gently shake out their hands. Now their feet, first the right, then the left, then both feet, while keeping the hands going, everyone should be wiggling and dancing energetically. Bring it back down.

Have everybody breathe again, for just a minute. Say: "While you breathe, make a package out of anything worrisome or bothersome that might keep you from the work today—the bad grade, fight with your boyfriend, fender bender, whatever. You can take the worry back later, but for now, put it in your package, tie the package shut, wrap it round with duct tape, and mentally levitate it out the door. If you need it later, it will be there for you."

Continue: "Everyone, see if you can contract all your muscles, tight, while you curl up, till you are still on your feet, but curled up tight in a ball. Now, even your face, make it as small as possible, tighten those muscles. Now release, stand back up, and reach again, for something different this time. Now come back to center.

"Now, close your eyes, and stand up straight. I want you to image that you have the point of a pencil coming out of the top of your head, at the fontanelle, where a baby has a soft spot, right where your skull knits together. This pencil point is contacting a sheet of paper above it. Now, keeping your body rigid, so from feet to top of head you form a straight line, draw a line forward on that paper, about five or six inches. Keep breathing!

"Great. Now back to center.

"Now draw a line backward, about six inches . . . and breathe . . . and back to center. Now to the left . . . and breathe, and back. Now to the right . . . breathe . . . back. Now you've drawn an X on that paper. Now, see if you can connect the points in a circle. You'll find places where the circle is flat, or jerky; just note this, and next time around, try to make the circle more of a circle . . . don't forget to breathe. Great. See if you can make the circle a little bit smaller . . . good. Try switching directions now. Make the circle clockwise if you've been counterclockwise, or vice versa. Don't forget to keep breathing! Great. Now see if you can slowly spiral into center, a little bit smaller on each pass, till you come to stillness . . . keep breathing."

When all have come to center, continue: "Great! Shake it out, and stretch out your face, as big as you can, while you shake out your hands, feet, arms, legs. Now make your whole face as small as you can, like a tiny little prune face . . . now as big as you can . . . keep breathing! Now, yawn. You'll naturally yawn, if I keep repeating the word. Feel how part of your throat arcs up, and gets big, when you yawn? That part is called the soft palate, and it controls how big the airway in your throat is. See if you can raise your soft palate without yawning. OK!"

lumpy ball game

Purpose: To create group focus and team building, provide a physical stretch, and energize

Group size: Fourteen max

Equipment: Crumpled paper wrapped in gaffer's tape (or duct tape)

Source: Adaptation of hackysack, popular schoolyard game; originally called D Ball (for "desire"), invented by the cast of a production of *Streetcar Named Desire*

First, you produce a lumpy ball, made of paper wrapped in duct tape, about three inches in diameter. Explain: "We're going to play hands-only hackysack, with this. It's paper, and it's fairly light. The object is to cooperate, so we keep the ball in the air as long as we can. Hands only—watch that you don't hit your neighbor— let's count how many hits we can keep the ball in the air. Great, let's try again. . . ."

guided imagery

Purpose: To relax, free the imagination

Group size: Any

Equipment: None

Source: Traditional relaxation method, authors are numerous

Having everyone lie down on the floor while you lead a guided imagery, or play a guided imagery relaxation tape, can be a great warm-up. There's a lot of material out there on these, so I won't include a sample here. Just make sure you do this when the group can avoid falling into a deep sleep. Monday should probably *not* be guided imagery day.

quickie sensory warm-up

Purpose: To free sensory apparatus

Group size: Any

Equipment: None

Source: I learned this from a fellow acting student many years ago, who cited Baba Ram Dass. Who knows?

Have students fold their hands. They will do it the way they habitually do it. The right thumb will be either on top or under the left thumb, depending on their habit. Now, have them switch the way they fold their hands to the other way. Feels weird, to some. Wakes up a new neural pathway. Shouldn't take more than thirty seconds of your warm-up. Avoid overprocessing.

the knot

Purpose: To build trust, energize

Group size: Fourteen max

Equipment: None

Source: Unknown

The group forms a circle. Now, everybody puts in one hand, finding another person's, and joins hands. Next, everyone puts in the other hand, finds a different person, and joins hands again. This is the knot. The group is to try to untangle the knot without letting go.

Observations It isn't always possible to undo the knot. There will be much exploration of stepping over, under, and through, as the group tries to re-form a circle. There's usually lots of laughter. Sometimes hands have to be readjusted, so that, for example, someone can rotate around. This exercise usually quickly identifies the "take charge" types; you may need to encourage them to let others have a say, or you may wish to have this be nonverbal. Monitor carefully to prevent discomfort or injury. This exercise builds a physical trust in the group as a group.

Set up the exercise such that it's understood that sometimes the knot cannot be untied; this is not a failure, if it becomes obvious.

ball of sound

Purpose: To create group focus, free vocal apparatus

Group size: Fourteen max

Equipment: None

Source: Unknown

The group forms a tight circle, as for The Willow in the Wind. They visualize the creation of a ball of sound, which is composed of their combined voices. It starts on the floor. The group creates, grows, and lifts the ball with their voices, until it floats up through the ceiling.

Observations This exercise should be repeated several times through training. It's important to give the group permission to fail: probably, in early training, this exercise will simply not work; do not belabor it. Go on to an energizing warm-up (such as the Knot or Zip, Zap, Zop) if it doesn't happen. This exercise demands and develops a higher group awareness of transformation through agreement; it releases players from preconceptions about their own voices. It should be first introduced after the group has some facility with space substance. As your group develops, so will their facility with this exercise, and there will be great joy the first time they solve the problem completely.

Setup "You are going to create a ball of sound, which is made of your combined voices. I want you to look at the middle of the circle, at the floor. If you all project your voices to that spot, all those vibrations will bisect right there, thus creating the ball of sound. Your task, as a group, is to create the ball, and cause it to float up, levitate, and finally disappear through the ceiling. See if you can make the ball, keep it whole, and lift it together as a group."

Sidecoach "See the ball as you create it together! Let yourself take a breath when you need to! Lift the ball with your combined voices! Don't try to force it!"

Discussion It's probably best to not discuss this much, save for reassurance, in the early stages. It may be observed that there may or may not be a correlation between pitch and the levitation of the ball: is there a paradigm that higher pitch equals higher levitation?

blind circle

Purpose: To build trust

Group size: Fourteen max

Equipment: None

Source: Traditional improv warm-up

The group makes a large circle and one player gets in the center. The center person (remember, you take the risk first) closes her eyes and walks in a straight line toward the edge of the circle. When she reaches the edge, the players gently turn her shoulders to point her in a new direction, and she walks again. Players should double-team, coming together so the center person may feel four hands instead of two.

Sidecoach If the center is very hesitant, say "Concentrate on your breathing; just walk normally as you take a nice, slow, deep breath and let it all the way out." If player is still hesitant: "I want you to do me a favor: while you walk, I want you to say the alphabet backward, starting with Z."

If center is walking in a curve, encourage a straight-line walk. As confidence emerges, encourage center to pick up pace.

If player is very assured and walking quickly, encourage group to keep their hands out in front when the center approaches, otherwise they may be kicked in the shins or have their feet stepped on.

If player is "cheating," say, "Remember that the goal is to have your eyes closed. If, involuntarily, they open, try to close them and stay with the focus of the exercise."

Observations This game can work very well outside, in a field or parking lot, but players must be warned to look out for variations in ground height so that they don't trip. As with all trust exercises, prohibit "jokes," such as spooky sounds or sudden grabbing. When a player has achieved an improved level of comfort with this exercise, call out "Open your eyes!" Players who have truly gotten into the game may be very surprised to see where they are.

Discussion Ask students how their other senses aided or hindered them in this exercise. (You probably don't need to discuss this much.)

clay molding

Purpose: To build trust

Group size: Any

Equipment: None

Source: Unknown

Variations: The Gallery

Players pair up. One is the "clay," the other the "sculptor." The sculptor molds the clay into a statue or an abstract sculpture.

A group member can lead all the sculptors, who have now become museum patrons, through the room on a tour, explaining pertinent points about the sculptures. (Hopefully, the tour guide will not be too long-winded, as holding the sculpture positions may become difficult.)

Next, conduct a group walk: All the sculptures, when completed, can "come to life," moving around the room (and each other) in their new shape, finding ways to move and interact as a result of the shapes they've been molded in.

Sidecoach "It's not about a scene, just explore your relationship to the space and the other players in this new shape. How do you move now? Where is your center? What is the voice of this new shape?"

Scenes Two pairs can work together, then on cue the two sculptures justify their positions in space in a scene, as in Three-Game Warm-Up.

This exercise is considered a trust activity because, for some, being "molded" is a difficult experience. Encourage gentleness and respect: look out for possible claustrophobia or inappropriate contact, particularly with a group you don't know well.

Advanced Exercises

silent/normal/overtalk

Purpose: To develop ability to use dialogue effectively in a scene

Group size: Two actors

Equipment: None

Source: Burns, incorporating Spolin's Silent Tension (Spolin 1999, 175)

Players who have an understanding of the Who, What, and Where can develop wonderfully engaging scenes with this. Remind (or introduce) players to the idea: In the scene, the silence between the players comes out of the tension between them, not an outside stimulus (example: husband/wife not speaking after an argument, as opposed to "in the library"). In all cases, the silence must come out of the tension, not an arbitrary "because that's the exercise."

Introduce "normal conversation": for the purposes of this exercise, it is conversation as it appears in written dialogue—one actor speaks, then the other. Tension should be maintained.

Introduce "overtalk": also, because of a strong tension, both players speak at the same time.

Run each of the three states with a pair of actors, to demonstrate. Sidecoach on What and Where as they do so.

When players understand these three states, have two players decide on a strong Who tension, a What, and a Where. They begin a scene with normal conversation. Sidecoach switching to silent tension, then back to normal conversation, then to overtalk. When players exhibit true facility, turn the switching over to them, by sidecoaching, "On your own" or "At will." (The cue should be established before exercise begins.)

Observations The players' goal should be to switch to the state called for as soon as the scene allows, but not arbitrarily. As with the silence in silent tension, the state called for must always be coming out of the tension. Therefore, at times there will be a brief lag between your sidecoach and the switch. Make sure they hear you: overtalk can be loud.

Tension is not always the result of anger or sadness: a new baby, an initial flirtation, and many other situations can provide the tension. Situational tension (don't wake mom while we raid the fridge) can be fruitful *if* it is relationship-driven. The tension must be powerful enough to drive all three states.

If a group masters this exercise, later in a rehearsal, a flagging scene can be revived by sidecoaching: "Go to Silent/Normal/Overtalk! Find the tension!"

Sidecoach "Remember the Where! Find a small object! Use all five senses! Talk with your feet in the silence! Talk with your back in the silence! Find a verb! Throw daggers with your eyes!"

Discussion How else did the tension show itself? Did it alter the space work? Was the Where a part of the tension? Were the actors performing or acting? How else does tension affect conversation?

chekhov

Purpose: To open actors to new ways of communicating on stage

Group size: Two

Equipment: Props, if needed by actors

Source: Burns

Two actors are in a scene, with a strong Who, What, and Where. Tell the actors that when you call out "Chekhov!" they are to each find something in themselves or in the Where—for example, their own heartbeat or a small object—on which to focus, which will cause dialogue to cease for a minimum of five seconds.

At first, actors should actually count this time in their heads, or you may count it aloud: "One alligator, two alligator. . . ." Be prepared to sidecoach with the counting if the actors resist a full five-second pause. Unlike Silent/Normal/Overtalk, the actors are to *immediately* switch to the focus and silence for five seconds, even if it means clamping the mouth shut in midsentence.

This exercise can seem very stilted and awkward for players at first. The arbitrary counting is necessary because it opens the player to an awareness of objective time on stage, which is often lost in the space of play. Calling "Checkhov!" at a point of tension or heightened conflict can force the verbal actor into new ways of expressing himself on stage. The actor who becomes very frustrated with this exercise initially should be encouraged to continue trying it; it can lead to a real breakthrough in onstage life. Experimentation with and repetition of this exercise can yield wonderful scenes. As with Silent/Normal/Overtalk, later in rehearsal you can sidecoach "Chekhov!" to energize (or slow down) a scene.

Discussion Did the players stifle a verbal impulse to comply with "Chekhov!"? Do people do that in real life? Did you see what they were about to say when they switched to silence? Did they say the same thing, five seconds later, that they would have said without the "Chekhov!"? Does this happen in real life? Is five seconds a long or a short time on stage? Is stage time the same as "real time"? Why or why not?

This is a good exercise to underscore the fact that the actor's frustration with the arbitrary "Chekhov!" may be seen by the audience as a deep, emotionally charged moment that is organically part of the scene: the audience knows more than the player does!

overwhelming greek messengers

Purpose: To work on advanced Who, What, Where, maintain a focus, prepare group for scenario building

Group size: Fourteen max

Equipment: None

Source: Burns

One player is the central character, who develops a Where and an activity. One by one, other players enter, establish (through action) a relationship, engage in the Where and/or a What (may be separate but related to central player's, such as eating cereal while central player washes dishes). Each of the other players lays a bombshell on the central player, by letting him know of an off-stage event that has a strong effect on the central player's life. After laying the bombshell, each player finds a reason to exit and is replaced by the next. The central player is to attempt to stay with the Where and the What and absorb the news from each Greek messenger while doing so. Bombshells should not be preplanned; they may build on each other or may be unrelated. After all the messengers have been on and off, the central player has a moment alone, thirty seconds or a minute during which the scene comes to an end. The central player is encouraged to find an ending that actively responds to the overwhelming series of messages from offstage.

Observations This is another arbitrary exercise and may not yield really effective scenes, but it is a very fun group game; young actors love it. Encourage involvement with the Who, What, and

Where. Sometimes, this can indeed yield very fine material; as a structure, it *can* be used to develop a scenario or a sketch. However, this is a tricky one: actors should be encouraged to stay with the reality of the scene, not to surrender to the impulse to go for the laugh. A relatively trivial, unconnected outside event that follows a major one can be a highly provocative choice, as it can demonstrate the way people really react (the bursting into tears over a broken dish after the death of a loved one for which little emotion was displayed is an example for discussion later).

Discussion Were the relationships clear? Did the messengers engage in the Where and a What? Was it plausible that the central player stayed with the scene and didn't rush offstage to react? *Could* it have been plausible? If not, why didn't player exit? (The answer "Because the exercise says to stay" can lead to a discussion of the rules/teacher approval versus obeying the theatrical reality. If this discussion ensues, be gentle with your central player.) Do people react logically to big news? Can you mourn the death of a loved one while continuing to wash dishes? What about the messengers? Did they show a real person conveying real news, or did the actors' glee pervade and undermine the scene's reality? How could this have been transformed?

topic machine

Purpose: To build scenarios (transitions)

Group size: Fourteen max

Equipment: None

Source: Burns, derived from Spolin's Part of a Whole

A topic or word is introduced. Actors create a machine using the sounds and the meaning of the word, as well as abstract movements/sounds suggested by the word. Example, using the word *Procrastination*:

Actor 1: Rhythmically repeats *procrastination,* with body motion that conveys indecision, but is repetitive

Actor 2: Comes in with second movement, word is *train station*

Actor 3: Adds a motion, rapidly repeats word *late*

Actor 4: Circles the others, chanting "Fiddle dee dee! I'll think about it tomorrow!"

Actor 5: Metronomelike motion, chants the changing time, as a time recording, thus: "It's seven fifty-four and thirty seconds. It's seven fifty-four and thirty-five seconds. . . ."

Observations This exercise demands a group that is comfortable with Part of a Whole (Spolin 1999, 73). The actors will also benefit greatly if you have worked as a group on basic rhythm building, using found rhythm instruments.

time dash braid

Purpose: To work on advanced Who, What, Where, build scenarios

Group size: Fourteen max

Equipment: Props

Source: Burns, derived from Shepherd's Time Dash

Three Time Dash structures are set up, with the goal that the three will be interrelated. Here's an example of a first Time Dash:

Who: Mother, son

Where: Kitchen

Times: Morning, after school, late Friday night

Second Time Dash

Who: Boyfriend, girlfriend

Where: School gym

Times: Mid-morning, mid-afternoon, late Friday night

Third Time Dash

Who: Policeman and teacher/husband and wife

Where: Car

Times: Early morning, midday, very late Friday night

Observations As laid out in the previous examples, the boyfriend-girlfriend pair could share a character with the mom-son pair; the son would be the boyfriend. But this is only the most obvious example. The group can work on this same bare-bones structure several times in workshop, with the following variations:

> The mother, the girlfriend, and the wife are the same person; the Time Dashes are separated by years, but similar events occur.

> The cop is also the boyfriend, the girlfriend is the teacher/ wife; again, Time Dashes would be separated by years.

In the case of these interlocking Time Dashes, the main characters will need minor roles to help tell the story, and the Brechtian devices of signs and announcements of where we are and when we are may become necessary.

props

A prop should be a tool but never a crutch. A hallmark of amateur acting is the stiff, unrealistic, panicked handling of props. In performance improv, the bare stage is the norm, and space work is king. Props tend to present problems, like how to put the real phone down on the space substance table. However, in an improvisationally *developed* piece, props can add richness and life to the work.

> *Purpose:* To free up actor's use of physical props, open the actor's imagination
>
> *Group size:* Up to twenty
>
> *Equipment:* Assorted hand props
>
> *Origin:* Combination of traditional improv training exercise and traditional improv performance game

This is a two-part exercise. The first part warms up the actors. In this part, you create a miniature proscenium, using an open door or an almost closed stage curtain. Each actor is given either a stick (such as a yardstick or pointer) or a scarf. The actor is to pass back and forth across the miniature performance space as many times as possible, with no hesitation between crossings, using the stick or scarf differently each time. For example, the stick could be used as a rifle, a bat, a telescope, a pool cue, and so forth. Encourage each new player to come up with new uses (rather than mimic those already seen) and have them alternate between stick and scarf. Your goal here is to push the group past its own perceived limits, to force them to come up with increasingly outlandish and imaginative uses for the stick and the scarf.

In part two, two pairs of actors work alternately. Each pair is given an odd hand prop—for example, an eggbeater and an oversize foam cowboy hat. As you call out to a given pair, they are to immediately come up with an unusual use for the prop, using any combination of gestures and words, in one short stroke. As soon as the pair makes its point, you call out the other group. This exercise should move very fast. The actors are encouraged to make visual jokes and use the props for anything but their intended use. After each set of four actors, introduce a new pair of props. Each pair should find a minimum of three to four uses for their props.

Observations If you see that one actor in a pair is dominating the exercise, you might want to shuffle the deck and have that actor step down, to give the more cautious actor a chance. Students should be reassured that not everyone is facile at this at first, but that everyone can do this exercise if they practice. Avoid overpraising the immediately facile actor.

The second part of this exercise is often used in performance by improv troupes, and it certainly stands alone. However, more important for your purposes, it frees up your actors' ability to look at physical props transformationally. Once this exercise is played and understood, while you are developing a theatre piece, the actors should have ready access to a prop and costume corner in your rehearsal space.

kitchen sink

Purpose: To introduce advanced ensemble exercise, build scenarios

Group size: Fourteen max

Equipment: Everything you have in the rehearsal space, including, if you have one, the kitchen sink

Source: Burns

Given a thematic or topical problem to solve, for example, a performance on addiction and the family, the group first discusses the theme or topic. When it is clear there is some real understanding of the theme or topic, a brainstorm ensues. The group comes up with a list of symbols or images that might illuminate the theme. Examples might be:

suffocation	victory at sea
spider's web	1950s sitcom: *Leave It to Beaver*
baby birds in a nest calling for food	bottomless pit
	dead end
multiple deadlines	warning light
a drunk driving a car full of kids	sinking boat

Actors then get together in a small group and attempt to weave as many of the images together in a music video–style montage as they can. Encourage actors to use any and all available props, lengths of cloth, costume fragments, signs, and so on, and to experiment with multiple foci/rapid shifts of focus. Further, encourage them to think of and apply sound effects, such as recorded music, to the montage. Story, as such, is unimportant; what is important is to create a theatrical composition that captures an essence of the topic or theme at hand.

Observations This is another workshop procedure that, with a well-developed group, may bring to life an amazingly detailed experience. My personal experience is that my role in this stage of development is to *get out of the actors' way;* once I have ascertained that they get the idea of this, I set a short time limit (say, ten minutes), then leave the room while they work. The feverish quality of the planning and the joyful and explosive quality of play that can result are truly wonderful. On the other hand, sometimes this exercise simply flops, which really is OK—it's another door leading into the group creative process, and sometimes it's locked.

This exercise can be combined with Time Dash Braids or with a single Time Dash, in a structure where a basic story is facilitated by the addition of nonlinear transitions and comments. Multimedia applications, such as recording and playing back video and audio snippets, can be a great addition to this method of developing a show.

opera

Purpose: To liven up a dying rehearsal process, shed new light on staging

Group size: Any

Equipment: Odd assortment of hats, scarves, costume fragments, and props

Source: Burns

If, in the course of developing a scene or a scenario, things seem to be getting cut-and-dried, or the actors don't seem to really connect with the material, the director calls out "Opera!," at which point all the actors are to rush to the props area, put on hats, grab outlandish props, and play their parts in imitation of Wagnerian opera. (Since it is likely that none of them will know the slightest thing about opera, Wagnerian or otherwise, you may need to coach them a bit.) The important thing is that they sing all their lines and find operatic/balletic ways of moving in the scene. Later, encourage them to keep whatever they found during Opera that might liven things up, as they go back to "regular" ways of playing the scene.

Observations This can test your commitment to process over product, as it is likely to lead to some of the most dreadful theatre you've ever experienced. But it can indeed wake up a sagging company. Be careful not to use this very often, or it won't work. It should be set up with the group in a quasi-conspiratorial way; let them know that they get to do it just once in a blue moon. They shouldn't know it's a remedy for lackluster performance, just that it's a fun thing that happens once in a while.

speed-through

Purpose: To energize a rehearsal, tighten a performance piece

Group size: Any

Equipment: All rehearsal props

Source: Traditional scripted rehearsal technique

Once a group has developed a scenario and a piece is well sketched out, sometime before the first actual performance, a speed run-through should be tried. Encourage actors to go through the entire piece, at triple their normal speed. I like to beat a drum or whatever is handy, to keep a rapid rhythm happening. Stress the importance of safety.

Observations Actors have a love/hate relationship with this exercise. It never fails to pick up a rehearsal and tighten a show. It also exposes weaknesses, brutally.

four square into ball throw

Purpose: To build actors' ability at dialogue, bolster volume

Group size: Any size; four at a time play

Equipment: Rubber playground ball

Source: Burns

First, teach the playground game Four Square. The game calls for four approximately four-foot squares, joined, to be drawn on the ground or floor. The result looks like a big square divided into four smaller ones. The game is rather like ping-pong: one player serves, by hitting the ball into another's square. The ball is volleyed; it must bounce once in a player's square before it is returned. When a player misses, she rotates out, and the next player takes her place. Players rotate counterclockwise as needed. If the server misses, he is replaced by the player opposite him. Soon a rather large group can rotate through. It's a great game because nobody wins forever, and everyone rotates out. Even the kids who are usually picked last on a team can be somewhat equal in Four Square.

Four Square has many, many ancillary rules, which are usually called out by name and agreed on by the players for a period of time. These rules serve to keep the game interesting. *Basic* rules may be found on the Web at <*www.tracy.k12.ca.us/afes/handbook /playground_rules.htm*>. It is quite possible that you or company members will know some of the ancillary rules.

After all have played the game, set up a dialogue scene, and give the players the ball to toss, roll, or throw back and forth with the lines. Encourage them to throw the ball in a way that connects with the emotion they perceive is appropriate for their character in the scene.

Sidecoach "Keep the ball rolling! Find a way to throw it to reflect the feeling! Punish him with the ball! Ask forgiveness with the ball!" (Use whatever verbs are appropriate.)

Observations Particularly with a younger or more tentative group, the playground game provides a tangible bridge into acting. The game rules make sense, as there is a paradigm already in place. The transition into the scene with the ball offers the tentative player a physical aid in expression. Later, the ball can be removed and other tasks substituted.

Stage Two Now, the ball acts as a builder of volume. Give the ball to the actor who has already played Four Square into a scene. Tell her to visualize a person about whom she feels a strong emotion, sitting fairly far away, and preferably up on something (in a gym, on top of the opposite basket works great). Ask her to say a fairly loaded but neutral line, while trying to hit the imaginary person with the ball. Line example: "You asked for this!" Encourage the actor to try several throws, perhaps with other lines, trying to hit the "person." Volume and connection with the line should grow tremendously. Encourage the actor to feel and record the physical sensation of the "big voice" thus produced. Later, you can side-coach the actor to remember this experience, saying, "Hit the person with the ball!"

Observations If you are working with an extremely angry actor, this one might let out some very large emotion—use caution.

☑️orks Cited

ALCOHOL AND SUBSTANCE ABUSE COUNCIL OF SARATOGA COUNTY (ASAC). 1993a. Arts Decentralization Grant Application. Saratoga Springs, NY. Unpublished.

———. 1993b. Asset Forfeiture Funds Grant Application. Saratoga Springs, NY. Unpublished.

AMERICAN PSYCHIATRIC ASSOCIATION (APA). 1994. *Diagnostic and Statistical Manual of Mental Disorders*. Washington, D.C.: American Psychiatric Press.

ARISTOTLE. 1978. *On Poetry and Style*. Translated by G. M. A. Grube. Indianapolis: Bobbs-Merrill.

BROOK, PETER. 1968. *The Empty Space*. New York: Atheneum.

FLANAGAN, HALLIE. [1938] 1973. Introduction to *Federal Theatre Plays*, by Pierre de Rohan. New York: Da Capo.

FOX, JONATHAN. 1991. "Die inszanierte persönliche Geschichte im Playback-Theatre" ("Dramatized Personal Story in Playback Theatre"). *Psychodrama: Zeitschrift für Theorie und Praxis*. Germany.

FREIRE, PAULO. 1987. "The 'Banking' Concept of Education." In *Ways of Reading: An Anthology for Writers*, edited by David Bartholomae and Anthony Petrosky, 238. New York: St. Martin's.

GLEITMAN, HENRY. 1991. *Psychology*. 3d ed. New York: W. W. Norton.

HANSEN, JAMES C., RICHARD W. WARNER, and ELSIE M. SMITH. 1976. *Group Counseling: Theory & Process*. Chicago: Rand McNally.

JOHNSON, DAVID W., and FRANK P. JOHNSON. 1982. *Joining Together: Group Theory and Group Skills*. 2d ed. Englewood Cliffs, NJ: Prentice-Hall.

LEVINSON, DANIEL J. 1978. *The Seasons of a Man's Life.* New York: Ballantine Books.

MCCROHAN, DONNA. 1987. *The Second City: A Backstage History of Comedy's Hottest Troupe.* New York: Perigee.

A Midwinter's Tale. 1995. Prod. by David Barron. Dir. by Kenneth Branagh. 98 mins. Castle Rock Entertainment/Sony Pictures Classics. Videocassette.

MILLER, ARTHUR. 1949. *Death of a Salesman.* New York: Viking.

MILLER, SUZANNE M. 1992. *Creating Change: Towards a Dialogic Pedagogy.* Albany, NY: National Research Center on Literature, Teaching and Learning.

OFFICE FOR SUBSTANCE ABUSE PREVENTION (OSAP). 1990a. *Communicating About Alcohol and Other Drugs: Strategies for Reaching Populations at Risk.* Prevention Monograph 5. Washington, D.C.: U. S. Department of Health and Human Services, Public Health Service Alcohol, Drug Abuse, and Mental Health Administration.

———. 1990b. *Stopping Alcohol and Other Drug Use Before It Starts: The Future of Prevention.* Prevention Monograph 1. Washington, D.C.: U. S. Department of Health and Human Services, Public Health Service Alcohol, Drug Abuse, and Mental Health Administration.

REED, LOU, and THE VELVET UNDERGROUND. 1974. "Heroin." *Rock 'n' Roll Animal.* New York: RCA. Sound recording.

Shakespeare in Love. 1998. Prod. by David Parfitt. Dir. by John Madden. 120 mins. Miramax Films. Videocassette.

SPOLIN, VIOLA. 1999. *Improvisation for the Theatre.* 3d ed. Evanston, IL: Northwestern University Press.

Waiting for Guffman. 1997. Prod. by Karen Murphy. Dir. by Christopher Guest. 84 mins. Castle Rock Entertainment. Videocassette.

WIMAN, RAYMOND V., and WESLEY C. MEIERHENRY. 1969. *Educational Media.* New York: Charles Merrill.